The Chelsea Football Book No. 3

THE
CHELSEA
FOOTBALL
BOOK No. 3

Edited by ALBERT SEWELL

STANLEY PAUL/LONDON

STANLEY PAUL & CO LTD
3 Fitzroy Square, London W1

AN IMPRINT OF THE HUTCHINSON GROUP

London Melbourne Sydney Auckland
Wellington Johannesburg Cape Town
and agencies throughout the world

First published 1972

This book has been set in Linotron Baskerville, printed in Great Britain by offset litho by Flarepath Printers Ltd., St. Albans, Herts. and bound by William Brendon of Tiptree, Essex

ISBN 0 09 112590 1

Foreword

by RICHARD ATTENBOROUGH, C.B.E.

There have been a number of momentous dates in the history of Chelsea Football Club, the vast majority of which appertained to events on the field. However, 5 June 1972 must, undoubtedly, take its place in our annals, since it saw the commencement of our tremendously exciting concept of the new Stamford Bridge Stadium. The ramifications are, needless to say, immense, since it must mean that, if our hopes are realised, we shall be the proud owners of one of the greatest Football Stadiums in the World.

I well remember, precisely thirty years ago, first watching Chelsea from the embankment on which there is now the West Stand. You can imagine, therefore, it is with enormous joy and pride that I am now a member of the Board deeply involved with this wonderful new development.

Obviously, the Stadium is as nothing if it is not matched by the dedication and skills of those on the field. With a manager of Dave Sexton's calibre and the players such as he has under his command, there can surely be no doubt as to what we may expect in the future, and I am sure that all the readers of this book would like to join with me in wishing them all possible good fortune.

Tomorrow's Stamford Bridge Comes Nearer to Today

Chelsea has always been a 'family' club, from the time it was founded in 1905 by the brothers H. A. ('Gus') and J. T. Mears, wealthy sporting gentlemen of the day. Down the years Stamford Bridge belonged to the J. T. Mears Trustees—until January 1971, when the club bought the 11½ acre freehold for £475,000. Under the chairmanship of the late Joe Mears, Chelsea won their first League Championship and more than doubled the stadium's seating capacity with the building of the West Stand, first used in season 1965–66. His son Brian considers himself the most fortunate Chelsea chairman of all to have been at the helm when the club won their first F.A. Cup, their first European trophy and now as the mammoth reconstruction of the 'family home' gets under way.

Brian Mears talks with understandable pride of the *new* Stamford Bridge when he says: 'Preparations for redevelopment began two years ago and it is to the delight of us all at Chelsea that plans have been launched which, when completed, will make this a soccer stadium second to none in Europe. We believe this is the biggest reconstruction ever undertaken at a British football ground, and reorganisation on such a scale cannot, of course, take place between one season and the next.

'Inevitably, it must be phased, and during the period of such a vast rebuilding programme there are going to be inconveniences to everyone—players and staff, management and, of course, the public. Supporters have waited most patiently for the long-promised rebuilding of Stamford Bridge, and now that a start has been made I am sure they will continue to bear with us while drawing-board plans are put into operation.

'For a long time we have realised that, for a club of our standing, facilities here have fallen short of standards else-

where. One particular problem has always been the distance between spectators and the pitch—how many trophies and points this may have cost Chelsea over thc years, we can only imagine.

'Despite this handicap, our players have won some of the game's biggest prizes in recent seasons, and the new design will bridge the gap and bring about a closer relationship between fans and players which we feel is highly desirable as we pursue further honours. I'm sure Dave Sexton and the players—as well as our supporters—will be pleased about this.

'The details of our new "super stadium" are as exciting as anything Chelsea Football Club has achieved on the field. The planning has been long and thorough because we wanted the end product to be exactly right. And now, as you can see, we are about to turn our dreams into reality.'

The unveiling of those plans, on June 5, made it evident to the most impatient supporter just why they had been so long in the making, for while many clubs have built modern stands, in Chelsea's case it is the building of a new stadium. The project, begun this summer, is phased for completion by the end of the Seventies at a total cost estimated at five and a half million pounds. When reconstruction is completed Stamford

How Stamford Bridge will look when Chelsea's £5½ million reconstruction programme is completed. In the foreground is the proposed West Cross motorway.

Bridge will accommodate all 60,000 spectators under cover. A likely breakdown (this has not yet been finally determined) is 40,000 of them seated and 20,000 standing, but all spectators *could* be seated.

Whether Stamford Bridge ever becomes an all-seater stadium depends on changing spectator habits; scope will exist for increasing the capacity to 80,000, if ever this should be felt desirable. Spectator safety and comfort is a high priority, with eventual provision of a wide double concourse system encircling the stadium which will be connected to entrances via ramps. This will provide for the smooth flow of spectators on entry and exit, and to assist crowd control and stewarding, pens accommodating up to 1,000 each are proposed.

The first stage, begun in June, is the construction of a two-tier cantilever East Stand, providing 12,000 seats. This is scheduled for opening at the start of next season (1973–74) and the cost is in the region of £1½ million. During the East Stand rebuilding period the capacity of Stamford Bridge will be reduced from 60,000 to approximately 52,000.

Since the stadium was opened in 1905 entry to Stamford Bridge has always been from Fulham Road. Now an important new access is proposed in the form of a direct connection from Fulham Broadway Underground Station to the North End of the ground. Up to 25,000 of a full-house 60,000 crowd will be able to take this covered approach-route from station to stadium, thus reducing by more than 40 per cent the near-total congestion that has regularly gripped the road network round the ground on big-match occasions. The new London Transport link will also remedy long-existing conditions whereby 60,000 pedestrians took over Fulham Road for 30–45 minutes after a game.

The East Stand will incorporate thirty private boxes, in addition to the six already existing in the West Stand, and when the whole development programme is completed the stadium will include 156 such luxury boxes, with service lifts and vehicle access.

The first (East Stand) phase is to include a Chelsea F.C. Vice-Presidents' Club which will be allocated five hundred stand seats, exclusive bar and dining facilities. Initially the Club will be restricted to 250 members, each entitled to two seats.

What else shall we see when all stages of redevelopment are completed? The pitch itself is going to be slightly larger than at present (115×75 yards compared with 114×71½ yards).

That will place the field of play exactly halfway between the upper and lower limits of International standard—indicating that Chelsea hope at some future date to challenge Wembley as the venue of England matches. The suggested new pitch measurements will provide another 474 square yards of playing area (8,625 compared with the existing 8,151). And to improve contact between spectators and players, the pitch will eventually be moved some 40 feet towards the North end of the stadium.

The existing 100 ft. floodlighting towers will come down and be replaced, as rebuilding progresses, by a side-lighting system mounted under the East and West Stand roofs.

It will be possible to incorporate in the design of the new stadium a system of warm-air heating of the stands, and with Stamford Bridge eventually closed in on all sides, investigation is being made into methods of inducing air currents to reach the pitch, thus assisting the drying-out process.

Inclusion of a large degree of glass on the roof and upper levels will not only increase the reflectiveness of the building and reduce its bulk and density within the rooftop character of the area; it will allow daylight to reach the pitch and reduce any feeling of oppression under the roof.

Other proposed facilities include a public restaurant; large indoor practice area for players—in addition, of course, to modern dressing-rooms, modernised physiotherapy department; new club administration block; two electronic information-scoreboards over the goal-ends; increased bar accommodation and toilets; new public address system; possibly a coach unloading/loading bay; closed-circuit TV facilities and eventually turnstiles linked electronically so that a crowd-count is maintained as spectators fill the stadium.

A valuable guide to spectator preferences was obtained from the questionnaire published in Chelsea's programme v. Leeds on March 27, 1971. This was how supporters assessed the suggested improvements that were listed:

HOW THEY VOTED

			Standing Adult	*Seated Adult*
1st	preference	All terraces covered	31.3%	26.2%
2nd	preference	Low-price bench seating	24.2%	21.0%
3rd	preference	Restaurant facilities	16.3%	19.9%
4th	preference	Club car-parking facilities	13.5%	17.8%
5th	preference	More licensed premises	10.5%	10.6%
6th	preference	Other activities	4.2%	4.5%

Chelsea's 'model' home as seen from above Fulham Road.

Response to the questionnaire provided information on the modern pattern of travel used by spectators at a capacity-attendance match. The 58,000 who attended Chelsea v. Leeds that day arrived as follows:

By car	25,621	Walked	4,048
By Underground	22,810	By coach	1,000
By bus	4,473	Other means	502

Analysis also indicated that 10,000 of the 58,000 crowd travelled between 25 and 75 miles to the game; that the number of cars driven to this particular match was 10,920—18% of the total attendance—at an average of 2–3 spectators per car.

Based on such figures, the *seasonal* use of transport facilities to Stamford Bridge on match days could be predicted as follows: by car 45.9%, Underground 36.5%, bus 7.9%, on foot 7.5%, by coach 1%, other means 1.2%.

Unfortunately, because so little land is available, only a limited amount of parking space can be provided within the main structure of the newly-designed stadium. (The study indicated that a match attracting 60,000 spectators involves 11,000–12,000 cars, and it is not feasible to accommodate

Goodbye, East Stand. The demolition men move in and prepare the way for the 12,000-seat cantilever stand which is due to be opened at the start of season 1973–74.

even a significant proportion of the parking demand—a multi-level car-park for half that number of vehicles would cost at least £6 million.)

In their questionnaire Chelsea invited supporters to submit their own ideas of stadium improvements. These could be classified in order of preference as follows:

1st Improved entrances and exits.
2nd Stands closer to pitch.
3rd Covered stands and terraces.
4th Improved toilets.
5th Electronic scoreboard; pre- and post-match entertainment.
6th Supporters' and social facilities.
7th More season-ticket facilities.
8th Boys' enclosures and entrances.
9th Improved public address system.
10th More low-price bench seating.
11th Direct link to Underground.

In Chelsea's desire to give their public what they want off the field as well as on it, it will be seen that many of the above facilities are being incorporated in the stadium's new design.

The inside view, showing terracing behind the goal and two tiers of seating above it.

The complete face-lift at Stamford Bridge, making Chelsea's famous home one of the finest sporting centres in Europe, will take us towards the end of the Seventies. But at last the wraps are off, Chelsea's exciting plans have been revealed, and a revolution in reconstruction is taking place before our eyes.

Whatever may be achieved on the field this season, supporters can already look forward to the start of 1973–74, when the opening of the new 12,000-seat East Stand will mark completion of phase one of this far-seeing plan to transform Stamford Bridge into a stadium of the future.

EDITOR'S NOTE: *I am indebted to Chelsea Football Club and Architects Darbourne & Darke for allowing me to reproduce above many statistics from the feasibility study carried out in the initial stages of preparation of the re-design of Stamford Bridge. The accompanying pictures of the stadium model were taken by Brecht-Einzig Ltd.*

In different ways, yet with everyone pulling in the same direction, the future rests with Chelsea's Board and Management every bit as much as with the Players. Standing: Dave Sexton (Manager), Richard Attenborough (Director), George Thomson (Director), Tony Green (Secretary). Seated: Lord Chelsea (Vice-Chairman), Brian Mears (Chairman), Leslie Mears (Director).

Wembley 1972

Chelsea went to Wembley on March 4 seeking a unique hat-trick following their 1970 F.A. Cup conquest and the European Cup-Winners' Cup triumph in 1971. Another question to be answered was whether they would become the first club to win the League Cup twice, their previous success having come in 1965 when the Final, played home and away, was still two years short of the clamour and glamour synonymous with today's big decider at the Empire Stadium.

Wembley was six months away when Chelsea played the season's first League Cup-tie, unpretentiously beating Plymouth Argyle 2–0 at Stamford Bridge with Peter Houseman's early header and the second goal shot at close range by John Hollins near the end of a match in which the brothers Ron and Allan Harris were rival captains.

In the League Chelsea were not yet averaging a point a game. Nottingham Forest, their third round opponents, were struggling even harder, but contrived two frights which left Chelsea glad of survival rather than over-optimistic about travelling full distance in the competition. With an hour gone Forest still led by McKenzie's first-minute goal, but David Webb, switched up front for the second half, forced a replay with a header. At Stamford Bridge, Forest again scored first and once more it took an hour before Chelsea were level. Then, Tommy Baldwin having shot the equaliser, Peter Osgood headed the winner three minutes later.

The fourth round brought Bolton Wanderers, seventh in the Third Division, to Stamford Bridge. That was another struggle, with Bolton ahead early on and Alan Hudson shooting the welcome equaliser just after half-time. Wembley still looked a long-odds proposition, the more so a week later, when unbelievable defeat in the Cup-Winners' Cup at home to Swedish part-timers Atvidaberg—or rather a 'technical knock-out' on the away-goal rule—plunged Stamford Bridge spirits to their lowest level in the four years since Dave Sexton returned.

With the season not yet three months old, the replay at Bolton was crucial. Pride was very much at stake, spirits needed to be revived quickly—and Bolton were on a hat-trick of First Division scalps, having knocked out Huddersfield 2–0 and Manchester City 3–0. Individually and as a team, a big effort was called for and, on the night, just about everything Chelsea attempted came off. Suddenly, all the pieces in the jig-saw fitted again. Charlie Cooke began the scoring, Tommy Baldwin helped himself to a hat-trick and there were two goals (one a penalty) by John Hollins, so that stay-at-home supporters were left doubting their ears when they heard among the night's results 'Bolton Wanderers nil, Chelsea six'.

Norwich City, setting the pace towards promotion from the Second Division, provided the fifth round opposition. On a wet, murky, mid-November night in East Anglia, Chelsea's defence stood firm under pressure—Peter Bonetti made two marvellous saves—and, from Peter Houseman's corner some twenty minutes into the second half, Peter Osgood headed the goal that settled a magnificent cup-tie.

The semi-final against Tottenham, the League Cup-holders, produced two classics. In the first leg at Stamford Bridge three days before Christmas, Osgood opened the scoring with a finely-angled shot (38 minutes) after a defensive mix-up, but directly after half-time the lead switched to Spurs, with Naylor and Chivers putting two in two minutes past John Phillips, who was in goal because Bonetti injured an ankle at Coventry the previous Friday. But Chris Garland equalised with a header—his first Chelsea goal—from Houseman's corner, and five minutes from time Hollins struck the surest of penalties (awarded for 'hands') to make the first-leg result 3–2.

Whether a one-goal margin would be enough was the subject of conjecture over Christmas, into the New Year and until January 5, second-leg night at White Hart Lane. There, in another splendid all-action match, Chivers volleyed the opening goal in first-half injury time. Garland equalised with a rocketing left-foot drive from 20 yards but, with only seven minutes to go, Peters levelled the aggregate with a penalty for 'hands' by Hudson. Could Chelsea come again? They could . . . and did. With extra time less than a minute away. Hudson hit a low free-kick from out near the left-wing corner-

Chelsea record-makers! The squad record their League Cup Final hit number 'Blue is the Colour', which climbed to fifth in the charts. Back row (left to right): Paddy Mulligan, Charlie Cooke, John Hollins, Marvin Hinton, David Webb, Peter Osgood, Chris Garland, Eddie McCreadie. Front row: Steve Kember, Tommy Baldwin, Ron Harris, Micky Droy, John Dempsey, Alan Hudson, John Phillips, Peter Houseman.

flag. It went 'through' everyone and into the far side of goal . . . and Chelsea were at Wembley 5–4 on aggregate.

In more ways than one Stoke City, second oldest club in the Football League, had taken their time arriving at Wembley. It was their first appearance in a Cup Final in their 109-year history, and they needed eleven games (compared with Chelsea's eight) involving 18 hours of League Cup football to get there.

While Chelsea were beating Spurs in two superb semi-final matches—and for one twenty-minute spell in the second leg playing some of the finest football ever to come from a Chelsea side—Stoke were locked in a four-game epic with West Ham. So never mind the grey skies and blustery wind on Final day; the 100,000 with tickets for the twelfth League Cup Final (the sixth at Wembley) sensed that if these teams could reproduce the quality and thrills that had carried them

Bolton were on a hat-trick of First Division scalps (they'd knocked out Huddersfield and Manchester City in the earlier rounds) when Chelsea travelled there for a fourth round replay. But the hat-trick went to Tommy Baldwin, and here's his second goal in Chelsea's 6–0 win.

through the semi-finals, then they were about to see a classic.

Chelsea were 7–4 on favourites, and there was endless theorising in the days of the big build-up. Wasn't it as good as a goal start that they were fielding eight men (plus substitute Tommy Baldwin) who had earned F.A. Cup-winners' medals against Leeds two years before? In the battle of youth (Hudson, 20, and Hollins, 25) versus age (Eastham, 35, Dobing 31) in midfield, would Stoke's 'old men' be able to last in Wembley's wide spaces? In Banks between the posts, Stoke had another of football's senior citizens, but an otherwise young defence would have to come to terms with Wembley nerves.

In hopeful anticipation, the open-bus drive and civic reception that had been part of Chelsea's Cup story in the two previous seasons were provisionally laid on for the following day. But Chelsea had suffered a damaging blow to morale the Saturday before, losing an F.A. Cup quarter-final place to Second Division Orient after being two goals up. What psychological effect might that have on them at Wembley?

We were not left long to find out, for within five minutes Stoke took the lead. As Harris attempted a clearance, the ball slewed off his boot and into touch near the corner-flag on Stoke's left. Dobing threw a long one; Bonetti's punch-out under pressure merely delayed the danger; Eastham returned the ball into the goalmouth, where Smith's shot cannoned upwards off Dempsey and Conroy headed in past the keeper's left hand.

Stoke had survived Chelsea's opening burst and grabbed their own first chance. But Wembley clearly suited Garland, playing the best football since his autumn arrival from Bristol City. From first whistle to last he ran aggressively, worked ceaselessly. He positioned himself to become Chelsea's principal target for the long ball aimed out of defence. Ever-eager, he refused to be intimidated by two clobbering tackles that put the names of Bloor and Pejic in referee Norman Burtenshaw's book in the first twenty minutes. Unless one totally misread the signs, here surely was a player destined to become a force in Chelsea football in the years ahead.

In those two incidents Garland was brought down just outside the area when in full flight for goal, but probably the real turning point came after 34 minutes when Mulligan, on one of his typical overlaps, crashed over the bye-line under challenge from Pejic. His studs had caught in Wembley's notorious turf which was extra spongy this early in the year, and

What a year for John Hollins! He was Chelsea's only ever-present player (58 matches), became team-captain and had his greatest scoring season with 18 goals. Eight of them were penalties, and this spot-kick in the closing minutes gave Chelsea a vital 3–2 win in the League Cup semi-final first leg at home to the holders Tottenham.

Chris Garland's best goal yet for Chelsea, as his 20-yard left-footer beats Jennings in the semi-final second leg at White Hart Lane.

The closing minutes were all action for Alan Hudson (above). He gave away a penalty for 'hands' and Spurs levelled the aggregate . . .

although Mulligan resumed after lengthy treatment from Harry Medhurst for the last four minutes of the first half, he disappeared from the match at half-time and spent all but the last 15 minutes soaking his badly bruised right ankle in the Wembley bath.

Chelsea paid doubly for Mulligan's injury, for the value of Houseman (who moved to left-back, with Harris switching to the right) was lost as a flank-runner getting the crosses in, and Baldwin's lack of match fitness after lengthy absence through injury was apparent almost as soon as he went on as substitute.

For some twenty minutes up to half-time, even while Mulligan was having attention and they were down to ten men, Chelsea kept Stoke under attack, and a minute before the break came the long-threatened equaliser. Cooke swung a pass diagonally into the penalty-area, where Webb lunged at it with his head, missed and, at the second attempt, knocked the ball to Osgood on the left. It was by no means the best chance that fell to Chelsea all afternoon but Osgood—booked only a minute earlier for a foul on Smith, his shadow—took it well, stumbling backwards as he shot and seeing Banks beaten more by direction than power.

That was the psychological moment for an equaliser, and as the teams went off for half-time a few moments later, not many inside Wembley would have gambled against the League Cup coming to Stamford Bridge. But chances made

With extra time only seconds away, Hudson's freak free-kick finds the gaps. They are all Spurs players in the picture, but Chelsea have drawn 2–2 on the night and won a Wembley place 5–4 on aggregate.

need to be taken—at least a percentage of them—and even giving Stoke credit for a stubborn defence, they did not always survive by their own efforts. Oh, for a fit Ian Hutchinson to have been out there, going for the near-post headers, pouncing on the penalty-area half-chance, instead of being still reduced by injury to his season-long role of spectator.

With 17 minutes left Conroy, running onto Dobing's fine pass, beat Harris down Stoke's left and crossed beyond the far post. Ritchie headed back, Greenhoff's shot was parried by Bonetti and Eastham swept the loose ball home—his first goal in two seasons. (In an era when it is hardly the done thing to attack with more than three men up, it is worth mentioning that all five Stoke 'forwards' combined in that winning goal.)

What remained was largely Chelsea versus Banks. With seven minutes to go, Osgood met Cooke's right-wing corner with a header so firm and true that it seemed bound to register, but Banks appeared out of thin air and glued his hands to the ball as it was going under the bar.

There was drama right to the end. Stoke's second corner of the match—against 13 by Chelsea—did not come until three minutes from time, and when it did Houseman headed Ritchie's header off the line. A minute into injury time Bernard's

A bad habit continues. As they did at Wembley in 1967 and 1970 Chelsea again concede the first goal, this time after only five minutes. Conroy's header is beyond reach of Peter Bonetti.

miscued back-pass was seized on by Garland, who went helter-skelter for goal. Banks rushed frantically from his line and, as Garland shot, we looked for the net to swirl, but somehow Banks got a deflecting knee to the ball, turned it behind and sent Garland crashing to the ground as they collided on the edge of the penalty-area.

So, for the third time in six seasons victory eluded Chelsea at Wembley. But they lost with style and spirit, and playing a lot of good football. Indeed, they had played better now, and lost, than they had done in the 1970 F.A. Cup Final, when they survived against Leeds at Wembley and then won the replay.

You could say the 1972 League Cup Final was a game Chelsea deserved to win and one they should never have lost; that Stoke were under enormous pressure for much of the match; that Hollins, Hudson and Cooke outpointed Stoke in the vital midfield area; that none of the luck went Chelsea's way.

And when you'd said all that, you knew in your heart that, as in the F.A. Cup at Orient a week earlier, Chelsea could blame no-one but themselves for getting the result so wrong after so much of the play right.

Would Chelsea have lost but for Mulligan's injury, which cost them width in attack with Houseman withdrawn to the back and broke the team's rhythm just when it was beginning

Peter Osgood is on the ground as he scoops the ball past Banks and, right on half-time, the favourites have drawn level.

But a five-forward move ends with Eastham winning the League Cup for Stoke. Too bad for Chelsea that he should choose this day to score his first goal in two seasons.

to flow? We shall never know. What we did know was that Stoke would never have won without those three wonderful saves by Banks—the first, seven minutes before half-time, when he pounced low to his right and held the shot that Garland had struck superbly on the turn; the second from Osgood's header towards the end and finally when he foiled Garland's last-minute breakaway.

No-one could begrudge Stoke their first trophy after 109 years of trying. Chelsea chairman Brian Mears put it like this: 'If we couldn't win today, there's no-one we would rather have lost to than Stoke City. The League Cup couldn't have gone to a nicer club.'

It's all over, and two great goalkeepers meet. Peter Bonetti congratulates Gordon Banks on his part in helping Stoke win a long-overdue first prize. Banks ended the season with further distinction—he was voted Footballer of the Year.

Dave Sexton said: 'Obviously we are very disappointed. But this proved once again that there is more to the game than playing well. Stoke did what we have done before—they clung on when they were being outplayed and still won, as we did when gaining our Cup successes in the last two years.'

For two years the sun had shone on Chelsea's cup football from a royal blue sky. Now, as was sure to happen sooner or later, it had clouded over. But even in the shadow of defeat against Stoke, nothing could detract from their achievement in reaching three Cup Finals in successive seasons.

Teams:

Chelsea (blue shirts with yellow numbers, blue shorts with yellow seam, yellow stockings): Bonetti; Mulligan (Baldwin), Harris, Hollins, Dempsey, Webb, Cooke, Garland, Osgood, Hudson, Houseman.

Stoke City (red and white striped shirts, white shorts and stockings): Banks; Marsh, Pejic, Bernard, Smith, Bloor, Conroy, Greenhoff (Mahoney), Ritchie, Dobing, Eastham.

Chelsea's Transfers Down the Years

Chelsea's first entry into the transfer market bought them three stars of the day for a combined fee of three hundred and forty pounds! The date was April 26, 1905. Chelsea had no team but, having decided to apply for membership of the Football League, they had to form one double-quick, and for their first signings they went to Small Heath (subsequently Birmingham). In a spectacular multiple transfer they bought inside-forward Jimmy Windridge for £190, centre-forward (later to become centre-half) Bob McRoberts for £100 and James Robertson, another inside-forward, for £50.

John Tait Robertson, a Scottish International half-back, had been appointed prospective player-manager pending completion of his contract with Glasgow Rangers, and with the League's annual meeting—at which Chelsea application for membership would be considered—only a month away, time was as precious as the players who were needed to make an impressive shop window.

The dramatic signing of Windridge, McRoberts and James Robertson told the football world that Chelsea meant business. It helped to persuade other clubs to part with class players, and signings that May included Willie Foulke, England's goalkeeping colossus from Sheffield United; full-backs Bob McEwan, from Glasgow Rangers, and Bob Mackie, from Heart of Midlothian, who also provided George Key to play at right-half; and from Manchester City came Jim Craigie to complete the half-back line with player-manager Robertson. City also supplied forward Frank Pearson, and among other front-line players signed were wee Martin Moran from Hearts, Spurs left-wing pair David Copeland and John Kirwan, and Tommy McDermott, from Everton.

The team thus assembled, Chelsea were ready for the Football League's annual meeting at the Tavistock Hotel,

THE FIRST CHELSEA TEAM OF ALL: Chelsea had no team only five weeks before they were elected to the Football League on May 29, 1905. But they moved swiftly in the transfer market and this was the "squad" they assembled for their first season of League football (1905–6), in which they finished third in the Second Division:—

Back row (left to right): J. T. Robertson (Manager), H. A. Mears (Founder & Chairman), M. Byrne, F. W. Parker (Hon. Financial Secretary), R. McRoberts, W. Foulke, D. Copeland, R. Mackie, J. Miller (Trainer), R. McEwan, H. Ransom (Trainer), A. Craigie, W. Lewis (Secretary), J. White (Assistant-Trainer).

Seated (middle row): M. Moran, C. Donaghy, T. Miller, Jas. Robertson, F. O'Hara, J. Windridge, H. Key, J. Kirwan.

Seated (front): M. Dowdall, A. Seaton, R. Wolfe, J. Walton.

Covent Garden on May 29. A few hours later the club which had yet to kick a ball had been admitted to the League, having convinced the meeting on three essential points: (1) Financial stability ('Gentlemen, we have more than three thousand pounds in the bank'); (2) Ground and accommodation worthy of a prospective First Division club; (3) The team was potentially strong enough to do itself credit against the majority of its rivals.

From £1,000 to £170,000

These have been the principal transfer milestones in Chelsea's history up to the end of last season:

Date	*Player & Position*	*From*	*Fee*
June 1907	Fred Rouse (IF)	Stoke City	£1,000
May 1919	Jack Cock (CF)	Huddersfield	£2,500
Nov. 1923	Andy Wilson (IF)	Middlesbrough	£6,000
May 1930	Hughie Gallacher (CF)	Newcastle	£10,000
Nov. 1945	Tommy Lawton (CF)	Everton	£11,500
Nov. 1950	Eric Parsons (OR)	West Ham	£23,000
Dec. 1961	Graham Moore (IF)	Cardiff	£35,000
Mar. 1963	Derek Kevan (CF)	West Bromwich	£45,000
Apr. 1966	Charlie Cooke (IF)	Dundee	£72,000
Oct. 1966	Tony Hateley (CF)	Aston Villa	£100,000
Nov. 1967	Alan Birchenall (IF)	Sheffield United	£100,000
May 1970	Keith Weller (F)	Millwall	£100,000
Sept. 1971	Chris Garland (IF)	Bristol City	£100,000
Sept. 1971	Steve Kember (IF)	Crystal Palace	£170,000

It is noticeable that all the above players were/are forwards, also that four of them figure in the list of Chelsea's record transfers *AWAY* from Stamford Bridge since the last war:

Date	*Player & Position*	*To*	*Fee*
Nov. 1947	Tommy Lawton (CF)	Notts County	£20,000
June 1961	Jimmy Greaves (IF)	A.C. Milan	£80,000
Apr. 1966	Terry Venables (IF)	Tottenham	£80,000
June 1967	Tony Hateley (CF)	Liverpool	£95,000
June 1970	Alan Birchenall (IF)	Crystal Palace	£100,000
Sept. 1971	Keith Weller (F)	Leicester	£100,000

Two years later, in the summer of 1907, Chelsea paid their first £1,000 transfer fee for an inside-forward named Fred Rouse, from Stoke City. On his first appearance for the Blues at Stamford Bridge, Rouse went down hurt, and as the Chelsea trainer dashed to his aid the opponent responsible for the injury received the admonishing cry from the terraces: 'Stop that—he cost Chelsea a thousand quid!'

That sort of sum is laughable now, when player-value is even more inflated than money-value. You don't have to be an England centre-forward of today to be priced in the £200,000 category—but in the summer of 1919 Chelsea bought the England centre-forward of *that* day, Jack Cock from Huddersfield town, for £2,500. What a bargain! Huddersfield were deep in the red, and it was said the cheque they received from Chelsea for Cock saved them from going out of business.

The fans were well pleased with the new capture. He scored two goals in his first match at The Bridge, against Bradford, and was Chelsea's top League marksman in season 1919–20 with 21 goals; next highest was Jimmy Croal with six. In his three seasons at Stamford Bridge Cock scored 47 goals in 99 First Division appearances before moving to Everton—marvellous value for £2,500. His successor, signed in November 1923 from Middlesbrough, was Scotland inside-forward Andy Wilson at what equalled the highest Football League transfer fee then known, £6,000.

Andy (not so mobile in 1972 but still following Chelsea closely last season from his New King's Road home and represented most match-days at Stamford Bridge by son Jimmy) could not prevent Chelsea going down to the Second Division at the end of his first season (1923–24). In the following five years they were tantalisingly near to coming up again, finishing 5th, 3rd, 4th, 3rd and 9th, and Wilson was still there to make a telling contribution when promotion *was* won as Second Division runners-up in 1930.

Having got back to the top class, Chelsea spent lavishly to make sure they stayed. In May 1930 they paid Newcastle United £10,000 for the finest centre-forward of his day, Scotland's wee Hughie Gallacher. Here was Chelsea's first ten thousand pound signing; the fee had been exceeded by only one previous deal—the £10,890 which Arsenal had paid Bolton Wanderers for David Jack in October 1928.

Chelsea did not stop at one big transfer. In June they bought another Scottish International forward, Alec Cheyne, from Aberdeen for £6,000, and three months later they spent £8,500 to parade Gallacher's Scotland team-mate, right-winger Alec Jackson, with him in the same club attack. Jackson, a star with Aberdeen at 17, had become king-pin of the best-ever Huddersfield forward line, and to bring the 'Gay Cavalier' to Stamford Bridge Chelsea bargained for days with the Yorkshire club before getting three thousand pounds knocked off the original asking figure.

By one of the quirks of fixture-making, in only his second game for Chelsea Hughie Gallacher found himself back at St. James's Park, playing against his old Newcastle colleagues. At the time of his transfer many Geordie supporters swore they would never watch the team again, but on his first return, on September 3, 1930, they flocked back to see the little

LAST SEASON'S RECORD SIGNING: Steve Kember's transfer from Crystal Palace in September 1971 sent the highest fee ever paid by Chelsea soaring to £170,000.

legendary figure—only five feet five of him and carrying less than eleven stone. Thousands were shut out and, to this day, the 68,386 crammed inside has remained the record attendance for St. James's Park. Only one thing spoiled the great homecoming—Newcastle won the match 1–0.

In just over four seasons and 134 First Division games with Chelsea, Gallacher scored 72 goals. Throughout his career he had to battle with his own quick-rising temper as much as with opponents, and there was at least one occasion when he asked to go off the field for a few minutes, to cool down lest he should lose his head.

Genius, eccentricity and unpredictable temperament were all part of Gallacher's box-office appeal, and it is interesting to note that when Chelsea transferred him to Derby County in November 1934 he went into the football record books as the most expensive player in the history of the game. In three moves he had cost just short of £20,000—£6,500 from Airdrieonians to Newcastle in December 1925, £10,000 from Newcastle to Chelsea and£3,000 from Chelsea to Derby.

David Calderhead, Chelsea's manager since 1906, retired at the end of season 1932–33. Leslie Knighton, who had been in charge of Birmingham for five years, followed him at Stamford Bridge, but it was Chelsea's next manager, Billy Birrell, who was to reign during the period of the game's most remarkable transfer escalation so far.

Birrell left Queen's Park Rangers to take over Chelsea in April 1939. Within five months the Second World War brought an end to first-class competition, and in the six seasons of 'utility' football that followed Chelsea were as dependent as the next club on guest players—stars on week-end leave from the Services or police, or snatching a few hours' break from work in munitions or other essential occupations.

The pay was thirty shillings a match, and somehow Birrell always managed to field a full side each Saturday—often thanks to response from the terraces to an appeal chalked on a blackboard and carried round the ground before kick-off asking 'If there's an outside-left (or whichever shirt needed filling) in the crowd, would he report to the dressing-room at once.'

Chelsea were already an ageing side when Birrell arrived, and of the pre-war players only Vic Woodley, Dick Spence, Peter Buchanan, Jimmy Argue, Dick Foss and Albert Tennant could still be considered as preparations were being made for 'normal service' to be resumed.

Chelsea moved swiftly to beat the market before it rocketed into the great nationwide rush to rebuild. The full-time transfer of war-time guest John Harris from Wolverhampton Wanderers was arranged at £5,000, and at a similar fee came England inside-forward Len Goulden from West Ham and full-back Danny Winter from Bolton Wanderers.

The biggest problem was that, for the first time in many years, Chelsea had no International to lead the attack. Birrell solved it in an equally big way, paying £11,500 to secure the reigning England centre-forward from Everton, Tommy Lawton.

THE FIRST MAN TO COST CHELSEA £10,000: That was Scotland centre-forward Hughie Gallacher, signed from Newcastle in May 1930.

BARGAIN BUYS AT £5,000 EACH: When manager Billy Birrell rebuilt Chelsea's team after the 1939–45 war, three of his finest buys were John Harris (left) from Wolves—he is pictured here in his modern role as manager of Sheffield United—Len Goulden (centre) from West Ham and Danny Winter (right) from Bolton.

That was in November 1945, the last season of the unofficial League South. The following winter brought the return of First Division fare. It was to be Lawton's only full season of League football for Chelsea, and when it ended in June, having been extended by unprecedented weather in mid-winter and the war-time ban that still existed on mid-week matches, he had set a new First Division record for the club with 26 goals.

Lawton had been signed at a record Chelsea fee and when he left exactly two years later, in November 1947, for Third Division Notts County it was at the new British record of £20,000, plus half-back Bill Dickson in part-exchange.

In a bid to counter the spiralling transfer market Billy Birrell started the Chelsea Youth Scheme in season 1947–48. 'The prices being asked and paid for footballers are getting out of hand, and it will get worse,' he said, adding in his shrewd Scottish way: 'We shall still have to buy players from time to time, but over the years we shall save a lot of money by raising many of our own youngsters.'

Chelsea could not wait, however, for boys to become men.

To rebuild the post-war side and at the same time keep their First Division place, they needed ready-made players—which was why Birrell bought forwards Bobby Campbell from Falkirk, Roy Bentley from Newcastle, Hughie Billington and left-back Hughes both from Luton.

In a matter of five years Chelsea's highest fee of £11,500 paid for Lawton had exactly doubled with the £23,000 signing of right-winger Eric Parsons from West Ham in November 1950. Parsons was to play a notable part in Chelsea's League Championship success of season 1954–55, but he made a luckless start with the club, developing cartilage trouble after only five matches and taking a long time to regain full confidence.

By the time Billy Birrell retired at the end of season 1951–52, only one product of Chelsea's junior fold had made a real mark in the First Division—Bobby Smith. But there was a steady flow during Ted Drake's managership from 1952 to

'TRANSFER FEES ARE GETTING OUT OF HAND', declared Billy Birrell in November 1945, after paying Everton the new British record fee of £11,500 to bring England centre-forward Tommy Lawton to Stamford Bridge.

CHAMPIONSHIP MAKERS: A big factor in Chelsea's League Championship triumph in season 1954–55 was the combined half-back strength of Derek Saunders (6), Ken Armstrong (4) and Stan Wicks (5). Says Ted Drake, who signed Wicks from Reading for £10,500: 'It was nothing short of tragedy that a knee injury ended big Stan's career when he was destined to become England's centre-half.'

1961, among them Jimmy Greaves, Barry Bridges, Ken Shellito, Bobby Tambling, Peter Bonetti and Terry Venables.

Indeed, Drake developed what is still Chelsea's only Championship-winning side without digging deeply into the transfer account. With young players of calibre coming through from their nursery, the club bought modestly during his reign. Drake paid only one £20,000 fee—for Coventry goalkeeper Reg Matthews; £12,000 was the figure at which he bought stylish inside-forward Johnny McNichol (his first signing for Chelsea) from Brighton, and giant full-back Peter Sillett from Southampton.

Ted, now travelling for an assurance and property company, lives at the same Wimbledon address as when he managed Chelsea. His fondness for the club has remained through the years since he left, and the affection is two-way—Ted was as usual prominent among the guests Chelsea invited to Wembley for last season's League Cup Final.

Of the players he brought to Stamford Bridge, Frank Blunstone belonged in the bargain-of-a-lifetime bracket. To sign the 18-year-old left-winger in February 1953, Drake made a road dash to Crewe after a tip-off that the Third Division North club might be prepared to part with their boy star. He arrived at the Gresty Road ground just as the board-meeting was breaking up, and to the question 'What are you doing here?' replied: 'I was driving past, saw the lights were on and thought I'd drop in and say hello. . . .' Within an hour the transfer had been agreed. Nine First Division clubs, Chelsea among them, had made previous attempts to sign Blunstone. If he had been placed on the open market, an auction could have developed. Instead, by moving in at the right time, Chelsea got their man for £7,000 . . and within two years Frank Blunstone was England's outside-left.

Ask Ted to name his 'best buy' for Chelsea and he hesitates between Blunstone and craggy centre-half Stan Wicks, signed from Reading (Drake's previous club) for £10,500 in January 1954. Says Ted: 'They were two great buys . . . tremendous players . . . terrific fellows, too, and it was a tragedy that both their careers were cut short by injury. Of course, we did see Frank at his playing peak, but big Stan—6ft. 2½in. and 13st. 3lb. of him—was finished by that knee injury before he reached his prime. He would have become the England centre-half forever and a day, like Jack Charlton did later on.'

During Drake's nine-year command, Chelsea's signings totalled no more than £155,000 in transfer fees (Steve

Kember alone cost more last season) and, with players sold for an aggregate of £250,000 during the same period, there was a profit of £95,000. Of that amount £80,000 came in one sale—that of Jimmy Greaves to A.C. Milan in June 1961.

Drake's successor, Tommy Docherty, was to become Chelsea's first 'transfer millionaire,' involving the club in deals to and from Stamford Bridge—that collectively came to £1,300,000 between the time he took over in November 1961 and his departure in October 1967.

Docherty's signings cost Chelsea £615,000 and the sales fetched £731,000, showing a credit balance of £116,000. The publicity value was beyond estimation, and at times the Doc manipulated the transfer market like a circus ringmaster. As the deals grew bigger, so did the headlines.

Four times he smashed the club's transfer record. It began with the £35,000 arrival of blond-haired inside-forward Graham Moore from Cardiff City in December 1961. In March 1963, with the prospect of first-time promotion back to the First Division slipping away, Tommy saw Derek Kevan as the quick-term answer and dashed to the Midlands to pay West Bromwich £45,000 for the ex-England centre-forward. By the Spring of 1966 Docherty was dismantling a Chelsea team that had only just missed greatness. New faces were on the way in . . . and the price of providing Dundee and Scotland ball artist Charlie Cooke with a peg in the Stamford Bridge dressing-room pushed the Chelsea record to £72,000. Six months later it soared spectacularly to £100,000 as centre-forward Tony Hateley was bought from Aston Villa to fill the gap when Peter Osgood broke his right leg at Blackpool in October 1966.

Under Docherty, Chelsea sold more players than they bought. The departure of Terry Venables to Spurs in May 1966 equalled the club's highest 'outward' fee of £80,000 and that particular record rose to £95,000 when Hateley moved again to Liverpool in June 1967. Chelsea's first £100,000 signing had lasted only eight months at Stamford Bridge, but while taking Osgood's place he headed the F.A. Cup semi-final winner against Leeds at Villa Park to take the club to their first peace-time Wembley Final and within two months Chelsea recouped all but £5,000 of their original outlay on him.

Hateley's was but one of a series of quick-fire 'in and out' transfers for which Docherty's reign was notable. In November 1961 he bought wing-half Andy Malcolm from

TOMMY DOCHERTY'S DEALS FOR CHELSEA

SIGNED

Date	*Player*	*Pos.*	*From*	*Fee*
Nov. 1961	Andy Malcolm	WH	West Ham	£12,000 (+ Tindall)
Nov. 1961	Allan Young	CH	Arsenal	£6,000
Dec. 1961	Errol McNally	G	Portadown	£5,000
Dec. 1961	Graham Moore	IF	Cardiff	£35,000
Mar. 1962	Dennis Sorrell	WH	Orient	£10,000
Apr. 1962	Eddie McCreadie	FB	East Stirling	£5,000
June 1962	Tommy Knox	OL	East Stirling	£5,000
Sept. 1962	Tommy Harmer	IF	Watford	£3,500
Oct. 1962	Jim Mulholland	CF	East Stirling	£8,000
Mar. 1963	Derek Kevan	CF	W.B.A.	£45,000
Aug. 1963	Marvin Hinton	CH	Charlton	£30,000
Feb. 1964	Barry Gould	CF	Arsenal	£2,000
June 1964	George Graham	IF	Arsenal	£5,000
Apr. 1965	Jim Barron	G	Wolves	£5,000
Nov. 1965	Tommy Robson	OL	Northampton	£30,000
Mar. 1966	Joe Kirkup	FB	West Ham	£35,000
Apr. 1966	Charlie Cooke	IF	Dundee	£72,000
May 1966	Allan Harris	FB	Coventry	£45,000
May 1966	Alex Stepney	G	Millwall	£50,000
Sept. 1966	Tommy Baldwin	IF	Arsenal	£25,000
Oct. 1966	Tony Hateley	CF	Aston Villa	£100,000
June 1967	Colin Waldron	CH	Bury	£25,000
Sept. 1967	Geoff Butler	FB	Middlesbrough	£57,000

SOLD

Date	*Player*	*Pos.*	*To*	*Fee*
Oct. 1961	Reg Matthews	G	Derby	£10,000
Nov. 1961	Ron Tindall	CF	West Ham	Part Exchange
Jan. 1962	Mike Block	OL	Brentford	£5,000
Jan. 1962	Sylvan Anderton	WH	Q.P.R.	£5,000
Mar. 1962	Gordon Bolland	IF	Leyton Orient	£8,000
Apr. 1962	John Sillett	FB	Coventry	£3,000
Sept. 1962	Mike Harrison	OL	Blackburn	£18,000
Sept. 1962	Terry Bradbury	WH	Southend	£4,500
Oct. 1962	Andy Malcolm	WH	Q.P.R.	£12,000
Oct. 1962	Peter Brabrook	OR	West Ham	£35,000
Mar. 1963	Mel Scott	CH	Brentford	£10,000
June 1963	Dennis Butler	FB	Hull	£10,000
Aug. 1963	Derek Kevan	CF	Man. City	£40,000
Aug. 1963	Colin Shaw	IF	Norwich	£5,000
Nov. 1963	Graham Moore	IF	Man. United	£35,000
Sept. 1964	Dennis Sorrell	WH	Leyton Orient	£3,000
Sept. 1964	Jim Mulholland	CF	Morton	£5,000
Nov. 1964	Dennis Brown	CF	Swindon	£17,000
Nov. 1964	Allan Harris	FB	Coventry	£35,000
Feb. 1965	Tommy Knox	OL	Newcastle	£10,000
July 1965	Ian Watson	FB	Q.P.R.	£10,000
Sept. 1965	John Mortimore	CH	Q.P.R.	£8,000
Oct. 1965	Jim McCalliog	IF	Sheff. Wed.	£37,500
May 1966	Terry Venables	IF	Tottenham	£80,000
May 1966	Barry Bridges	CF	Birmingham	£55,000
Aug. 1966	Bert Murray	OR	Birmingham	£25,000
Sept. 1966	Alex Stepney	G	Man. United	£50,000
Sept. 1966	George Graham	IF	Arsenal	£50,000
Dec. 1966	Tommy Robson	OL	Newcastle	£20,000
June 1967	Tony Hateley	CF	Liverpool	£95,000
July 1967	Allan Harris	FB	Q.P.R.	£30,000

West Ham for £12,000 (plus Ron Tindall); in October 1962 Malcolm joined Queen's Park Rangers for £12,000. In November 1963 Docherty sold Graham Moore to Matt Busby to retrieve from Manchester United the £35,000 he had paid Cardiff two years before. Dennis Sorrell, Orient wing-half signed for £10,000 in March 1962, went back to Leyton for £3,000 in September 1964.

Derek Kevan, bought for £45,000 from West Bromwich in March 1963, was on his way again—to Manchester City—only five months later for all but £5,000 of what he had cost Chelsea.

CHELSEA'S MOST EXPENSIVE SCOT: The description still fits Charlie Cooke, who cost £72,000 from Dundee in April 1966.

Even more extraordinary was the triple transfer of full-back Allan Harris in which Chelsea were involved in less than three years. In November 1964 they let him go to Coventry City for £35,000 . . . in May 1966 they bought him back for £45,000 . . . and in July 1967 Harris became the last entry in Docherty's 'Chelsea sales' ledger, transferred to Q.P.R. for £30,000.

Perhaps the Doc's most astonishing deal concerned goal-keeper Alex Stepney. He was bought from Millwall for £50,000 in May 1966, and the football grapevine had it that room would be made for Chelsea's new No. 1 by letting Peter Bonetti go to West Ham. But it was Stepney who moved on—only four months (and one First Division appearance) after he'd arrived at Stamford Bridge. He went to Manchester United for the £50,000 Chelsea had paid for him. Docherty had done it again!

In October 1967 Chelsea's team managership passed to Dave Sexton. His arrival brought greater stability to the club's transfer-market activities—and still more expensive newcomers to the team-sheet. The big difference was that whereas Docherty beat the transfer drum like few managers before or since, Sexton moved quietly about his business and was often still reluctant to talk much about a six-figure signing even after the deal was sealed.

Within a month of his appointment Dave spent £100,000 on striker Alan Birchenall, from Sheffield United. Within days of Chelsea winning the F.A. Cup for the first time in May 1970, he swooped on Millwall and bought Keith Weller for £100,000 . . . and he recovered the money a month later with the sale of Birchenall to Crystal Palace.

In September 1971 Chelsea paid more than a quarter of a million pounds for two new forward stars—Chris Garland from Bristol City for £100,000 and Steve Kember from Crystal Palace for another new record Chelsea fee of £170,000. That month the transfer of Weller to Leicester City fetched back £100,000.

Dave Sexton's star signings have not all cost six-figure sums. In recent times there haven't been many better £40,000 buys than David Webb from Southampton, and how Paddy Mulligan's value must have soared since Chelsea paid Shamrock Rovers £17,500 for him in October 1969. Then there's Ian Hutchinson—£2,500 down when Chelsea signed him from Cambridge United, another £2,500 after a dozen League games and, within two years, valued at £100,000.

DAVE SEXTON'S BIGGEST BARGAIN? Only time will tell, but already Republic of Ireland defender *Paddy Mulligan* has more than repaid the £17,500 which Shamrock Rovers asked for his transfer in October 1969.

THIS IS THE PLACE FOR ME, says Chris Garland as he sets foot in the Chelsea dressing-room on the day of his £100,000 transfer from Bristol City.

By the time Kember was signed in September 1971, Dave Sexton's turnover in the transfer market on Chelsea's behalf topped £1,100,000 with signings costing £634,000 and sales totalling just under £500,000.

At that point Chelsea had signed more £100,000 footballers (five—Hateley, Birchenall, Weller, Garland and Kember) than any other club. Over a period of ten years, from August 1961, they had been soccer's biggest buyers with £1,262,000 spent on new players (followed by Spurs at £1,200,000 and Newcastle third, some £50,000 behind). How well the Stamford Bridge transfer budget has been balanced is shown by the fact that Chelsea also topped the 'league of big sellers,' having received £1,237,000 from the sale of players over the same ten years.

Nobody could remotely have visualised the way the transfer trail would develop that day in April 1905 when it all began with the signing of the club's first three players for a mere three hundred and forty sovereigns. Just as we can only dream now of the heights which transfer fees will reach over the next ten, twenty years and into the next century. You may be sure that with a magnificent new stadium now under construction, Chelsea will keep pace on the field. Great arenas demand great teams to fill them, and by the end of the Seventies Chelsea mean to have both.

DAVE SEXTON'S CHELSEA TRANSFERS

SIGNED

Date	*Player*	*Pos.*	*From*	*Fee*
Nov. 1967	Alan Birchenall	S	Sheff. Utd.	£100,000
Feb. 1968	David Webb	CB	Southampton	£40,000
July 1968	Ian Hutchinson	CF	Cambridge Utd.	£5,000
Jan. 1969	John Dempsey	CB	Fulham	£70,000
Oct. 1969	Paddy Mulligan	FB	Shamrock Rov.	£17,500
Nov. 1969	Ian Delacour	FB	Portadown	£4,500
May 1970	Keith Weller	S/M	Millwall	£100,000
Aug. 1970	John Phillips	G	Aston Villa	£25,000
July 1971	Kevin Barry	S	Hastings	£2,000
Sept. 1971	Chris Garland	S	Bristol City	£100,000
Sept. 1971	Steve Kember	M	Crystal Palace	£170,000

SOLD

Date	*Player*	*Pos.*	*To*	*Fee*
Oct. 1967	Colin Waldron	CB	Burnley	£30,000
Jan. 1968	Geoff Butler	FB	Sunderland	£65,000
Feb. 1968	Joe Kirkup	FB	Southampton	£30,000
Sept. 1968	Ian Hamilton	S/M	Southend	£5,000
Sept. 1968	Jim Thomson	CB	Burnley	£40,000
Jan. 1969	Allan Young	CB	Torquay	£8,000
Jan. 1969	Barry Lloyd	M	Fulham	£30,000
June 1970	Alan Birchenall	S	Crystal Palace	£100,000
June 1970	Bobby Tambling	S	Crystal Palace	£40,000
May 1971	Tommy Hughes	G	Aston Villa	£12,500
July 1971	Alan Dovey	G	Brighton	£1,000
Sept. 1971	Derek Smethurst	M	Millwall	£35,000
Sept. 1971	Keith Weller	S/M	Leicester	£100,000

David Webb

Chuffed when we win, choked when we lose—that's me, whether I'm playing five-a-sides on Friday morning in the Stamford Bridge forecourt or Cup Finals at Wembley, Old Trafford or in Athens. After our big successes the two previous years, it hit all the harder when the various cups gave Chelsea the elbow last season. Even now when I think about it, I still can't believe it.

I ask you! First, We're dumped out of Europe by a bunch of part–timers from Sweden called Atvidaberg. Then we're knocked out of the F.A. Cup after being two up away to Second Division Orient. That really cut me up, I can tell you, on the ground where I began my career. After the game I went to my mother-in-law's place a few streets away and sat staring at my supper all night. Numb, I was.

Then, blow me, a week later we're done by Stoke at Wembley. Good luck and all that to them—they'd been trying to win something for more than a century—but they weren't exactly in the class of Leeds or Liverpool or Arsenal, were they? Or ours . . . on any other day.

If anyone had suggested at the start of last season that we were going to lose our way in those three cups to teams like Atvidaberg, Orient (meaning no disrespect, 'cause I'll always have great affection for my first club over there in East London) and Stoke, I'd have fallen down laughing. But it happened. Don't ask me to explain how. It just did. Maybe we were a bit complacent about the Swedes, and we certainly lost concentration and paid for it against the O's. Stoke? Let's just say I hope we're playing them in another Final this season!

All I know is that that League Cup Final defeat left a scar on my heart, and it'll be there until we win another big prize. But by the end of the season you fans had me bouncing again when you voted me Chelsea's 'Player of the Year' for the

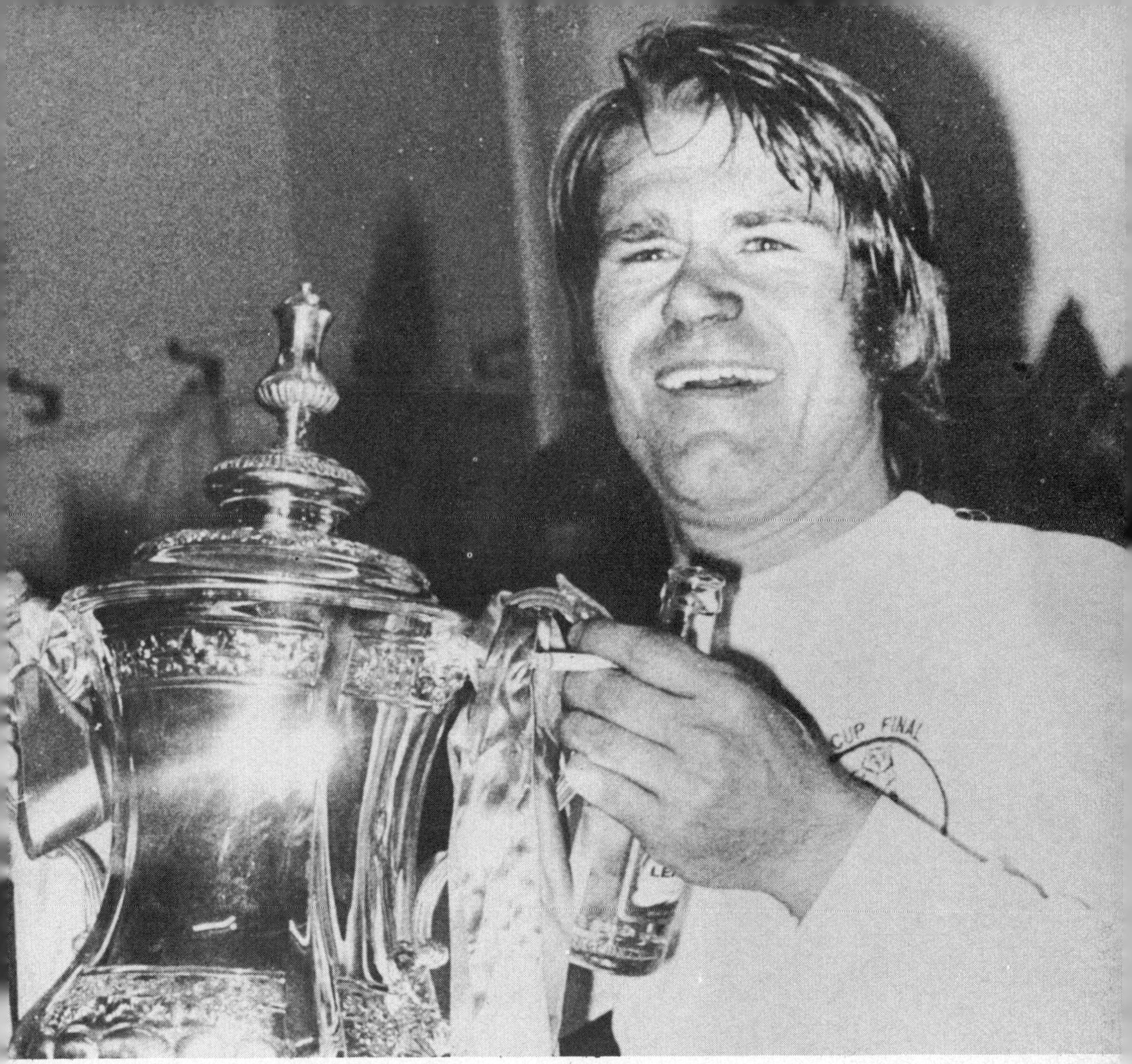

second time. I felt terrifically honoured and, unlike the rest of the lads, I had something to put against the season's disappointments.

Up to the start of this season I'd chalked up more than 200 first-team games in four and a bit seasons with Chelsea and about 350 League appearances in my career . . . and I'm still only a slip of a lad! Yes, I know all about the ups and downs of being a professional footballer, and even among so many matches some dates really stick out in my mind.

Even in a Leeds shirt, Dave still looks right to Chelsea fans with that Cup in his hands.

He'll never have a greater moment than this—Webb's extra-time header that beat Leeds in the 1970 F.A. Cup Final replay at Old Trafford.

Like Saturday, March 2, 1968—my first game for Chelsea. We were away to Manchester United, and we beat 'em 3–1. I knew then that I'd become part of a soccer set-up that was going places, and that's exactly how it has worked out.

Going places like Athens in May last year, when we were one-all after extra time against the fabulous Real Madrid in the Final of the European Cup-Winners' Cup. Then hanging around the Greek capital for a couple more days awaiting the replay and finally lifting Chelsea's first European trophy by 2–1.

Like going to Wembley the previous year, and yours truly getting a right old run-around from Eddie Gray, of Leeds United, and that Cup Final ending at 2–2, extra time and all. Then going on to Old Trafford, Manchester, and me in the news this time for the right reason and heading the goal that brought Chelsea the F.A. Cup for the first time in the club's long history.

And all the other places I've seen and sampled in European competitions and on close-season tours. Chelsea certainly go places in more ways than one.

Signing for Chelsea was the best move I ever did make. I mean that from the bottom of my heart. For a start, I'm a Londoner born and bred, and I'm sure I could never really settle down anywhere else. I tried at Southampton, where I had two years and 75-odd games.

Before that I'd done the rounds, as they say, in London. As a kid I was West Ham barmy—my Dad was, too. I used to go along and see their stars, like Noel Cantwell and Frank O'Farrell, and dream of the day when I was a professional. I'll always remember my Dad's last words to me before he died: 'Keep up your football, son.'

We were a big family (I have five sisters and two brothers) and kids need feeding, but money was tight so I left school early and got a job as an office junior with the London Co-op. Football filled my week-ends—I played Saturday morning and afternoon, Sunday morning and afternoon.

From West Ham juniors I'd dash off for a Saturday afternoon game somewhere else. Sundays I played for a pub side called the 'Angels' on Hackney Marshes. I've carried the goalposts through the mud and slosh across those fields with the best of 'em.

It didn't take me long to see I'd never make it at Upton Park. Everywhere I looked, there was a queue of class defenders—and I've never claimed to be one of those. So I moved down the road to Orient. The bloke who gave me my chance there is now here at Chelsea—Eddie Heath, who is Ken Shellito's right-hand man in the Youth section.

At that time he was running Orient's juniors. I figured I must have a better chance of making it with a smaller club like the O's, and worked at it. Johnny Carey was manager then, and he was the fellow who made me a professional at Leyton. I signed for ten quid a week, and felt like a millionaire after being a £3 17s.-a-week clerk.

But those 18 months working for the Co-op were all good experience. More than anything else, they taught me the value of money. I'd grown up to appreciate the pennies and tuppences, so, excited as I was at the chance to make football a career, being on a tenner a week didn't turn my head. Even now, it does no harm to remember the rough times. Yes, I still know where I came up from.

Dave Sexton had been a player at West Ham. When he went into management, I played under him at Orient . . . and it was Dave who pulled me back from Southampton to London, where my roots have always been. When I made my first appearance at Stamford Bridge, I knew I was really home. It gave me a tremendous thrill to hear the Shed chanting my name . . . 'David Webb, David Webb.' I still feel about ten feet tall when I hear it, and that kind of support really pushes you on.

I've never put myself up as a player who has all the skills. But I know I'm a trier. Tackling and heading are my strong points, and I try to read the game . . . see, almost in advance, what's going to happen.

Memories? I've got a stack of them, besides our Cup successes . . . and Cup shocks. Like getting a hat-trick away to Ipswich on Boxing Day 1968 while wearing the No. 5 shirt. My wife, Jackie, has never really got over that. They flashed my face on the television screen that night and she immediately thought I'd been sent off.

Since then I've worn the No. 9 shirt—and a whole washing-line of others, too—and enjoyed myself immensely up front. And there was that fantastic afternoon last season when I played the whole 90 minutes in goal. That was another Christmas game against Ipswich, but this time at The Bridge.

I've had enough excitement with Chelsea to last most folk a life-time, and the biggest influence of all on my career has been Manager Dave Sexton. I've not come across anyone who thinks as deeply as he does about the game. His last words before every away match must have been worth a helluva lot of points to Chelsea. He always tells us: 'It's *their* ground we've come to. It's *their* pitch we're playing on. But it's not *their* ball?' When you think about it, that's quite some approach, isn't it? Yes, for what I've already achieved in the game, and for anything I may achieve in the future, I owe Dave Sexton a load of thanks.

Being with other clubs did me good, helped me appreciate just how good the set-up is at Stamford Bridge. How could I complain about anything, when I'm being paid to do the job I like best and I'm doing it with a club that really is going places?

We've got the players and the organisation to get a big grip

The longest two and a half hours of my life. That's how David Webb described his spell as Chelsea's First Division goalkeeper last December. First, he took over for an hour when Peter Bonetti injured an ankle in a Friday night match at Coventry. Ten days later, on Boxing Day, with no one else available, Dave played the whole game at home to Ipswich in goal . . . kept a clean sheet, too. Here he is in action during that 2–0 win.

on things, and for me the League title remains one huge ambition. Every bit as important is that we've got the supporters, the fans, the fanatics. To every one of them I'd just like to say: Thanks a lot for everything—your support, your matiness, your encouragement.

Editor Albert Sewell writes: It wasn't only Chelsea Player of the Year statuette that David Webb received again last season (he previously won it in 1968-69). At various times he has collected a total of twenty stitches in different head wounds, the worst in January 1971 in the home game against Manchester United. When the club doctor had finished the needlework after the match Dave—Chelsea's Desperate Dan, he has been called—shook his sore head and cracked: 'I'm honoured. There can't be anyone else in football who can claim to have had eight stitches out of a bump with Bobby Charlton!'

Two hairy moments in the life of Chelsea's 'Desperate Dan'. Left: At a Sportsman Club reception after the F.A. Cup win in May 1970. Right: The Wembley shampoo treatment just before last season's League Cup Final.

Webb collects shirts as well as stitches. By playing a full-length match in goal at home to Ipswich on Boxing Day, and three months later in the role of emergency striker, he raised the total of different shirts he has worn in the cause of Chelsea to ten. They were numbers 1 to 9 inclusive and the substitute's 12. It was no surprise that one devoted fan should write to Chelsea and ask: 'Is it true that when the players made

Away from it all: If David Webb had not become a soccer star, he might well have made his name as a speedway ace. You can tell that from the style! What, no crash helmet? 'I always wear one on the bike—except when I'm having my picture taken,' says Dave. And with all the stitches he's collected from his football injuries, it might not be a bad idea if he wore a crash helmet on the pitch, too!

their hit record "Blue is the Colour" David Webb sang all the voices?'

When you list the qualities of Webb's football, you talk of dedication, determination, application, inspiration, spirit, versatility and unceasing endeavour . . . and there's still another major ingredient to add. It is one that is reciprocated by the fans—the obvious enjoyment he gets from his game.

How they loved it when he knelt in make-believe prayer at the foot of the post before keeping goal in that game against Ipswich, when Peter Bonetti and John Phillips were both injured and third-choice Steve Sherwood arrived just too late to make his debut after a road dash from Yorkshire, where he was spending Christmas with his family. And how the applause rolled round the ground as Webb dived at an opponent's feet and diverted the ball over the bar to keep a clean sheet at one end while Steve Kember and Chris Garland scored at the other.

Webb had also worn the 'keeper's jersey for an hour at Coventry in the previous League game after Bonetti damaged an ankle. But this first experience of playing goalkeeper in the First Division came with Southampton in season 1966-67. After about ten minutes Campbell Forsyth broke a leg against Liverpool. No provision had been made for such an emergency, and Ted Bates told Dave to go in goal. He did well, too, but Liverpool won 2–1.

David Webb is assured of a permanent place in the hearts of Chelsea fans. As a players' player and a manager's player, too, he is well summed up in these words of Dave Sexton: 'Webby is some fellow to have in your side . . . anywhere. He's always had flair, and his whole attitude is so very good—a born competitor with enormous enthusiasm. He puts a lot of thought into his game. You can see that in training and off the field too. He goes to other clubs' matches, seeing what ideas he can pick up, and has helped himself become a better player by his willingness to learn.'

By his own description, Webb is a 'rough and ready looking geezer.' It would be hard to improve on what Ray Connolly wrote in his celebrity-interview in the *Evening Standard* series last season: 'Physically he's what you might call a big rough-looking lad with a face more remarkable for its character than its sensitivity; the nose fleshy and upturned like a cheeky blob of putty; the dimple in the chin which looks as though it might have been quarried with a pick-axe; and a worry-line across the forehead that looks like a rock-rift caused by some earthquake inside his skull. . . .

'So really he's a formidable-looking object out there in Chelsea's defence every Saturday afternoon, and the terraces this season have adopted him as their favourite son. All the world loves a trier, and Webb never stops trying and working and larking about a bit, too, when the mood takes him. . . .'

The mood to become a professional footballer took Dave by the time he was twelve. He remembers: 'What really decided me was coming 28th in a class of 30—the other two hadn't taken the exams because they'd been off ill. The headmaster asked me what I wanted to be. When I said "a footballer", he laughed and asked if I'd ever heard of Stanley Matthews. "Yes, sir", I replied, and he said, "Well, he uses his brains as well as his feet. You'll never be a footballer." That was just the gee-up I needed. It only made me want to play all the more. If I wore a hat, I'd take it off to that headmaster. Without the challenge he threw out, I can't begin to think what I might otherwise be doing now.'

David Webb—Personal File

Birthdate: 9.4.46.
Birthplace: Stratford.
Height: 5ft 11¼in.
Weight: 13st. 4lb.
Colour of hair: Light brown.
Colour of eyes: Blue.
Wife's name: Jackie.
Present home: Chigwell, Essex.
Outside interests: Football kit-cleaning business (Kleen-a-Kit)—partner is John Dempsey.
Hobbies: Meeting people . . . visiting interesting places . . . coaching.
Footballers he most respects: Dave Mackay, Derek Dougan, Martin Chivers, Frank McLintock.
Other sportsmen he admires: Barry Bridges (Speedway), John Surtees, Jackie Stewart.
Car: Audi.
Family pet: Alsatian named Cobb (Cobb-Webb!)
Biggest thrills of career: Scoring the F.A. Cup-winning goal against Leeds (1970) and the King's Road welcome home next day.
Favourite away grounds: West Ham and Manchester United.
Other 'favourites': Colour—blue; Food—anything; Drink—Double Diamond; Clothes—King's Road style; Singers—James Taylor, Carole King; Groups—Carpenters, Beatles, Rolling Stones; Actors—Michael Crawford, Tony Curtis.
Boyhood ambitions: Until 12, to be a speedway rider; after that, professional footballer.
Career ambition: To do well in a Chelsea team that becomes so powerful we feel we can never be beaten.

My Chelsea Cavalcade

by GEOFFREY GREEN *(The Times)*

For half a century now I've had a lover's quarrel with Chelsea: unable to live with, or without, 'her'. About 1922, as a snotty-nosed youth of 11 years, with a sixpenny piece in one pocket and a grubby bag of liquorice in the other, I first went to Stamford Bridge. To be accurate, an uncle took me. Having arrived on these shores from India only a couple of years earlier, this was my introduction to English football of the 'big time'.

It wasn't the 'big time' of today, of course. The crowds were just as big—probably bigger on occasion—but the whole game was set in a lower gear. Socially, soccer was frowned upon as a sport largely for the working classes. Professionalism was a dirty word for the gentry.

That was one thing. Another was that football was still a long way from being exploited commercially, as it is now. There were rosettes and rattles to be bought down the Fulham Road, or outside Walham Green Station, as it was then. But there were no supporters' clubs; no gangs of fans moving like noisy locusts across the city; no busting up of trains and local shop windows; no vandalism; no singing on the terraces; no selling of a myriad knick-knacks such as has now grown to be the by-product of football, a specialised trade of its own.

The crowds cheered, naturally, and rattles whirred. But, compared with the present, it was all rather prim. Hysteria and a running fever were largely unknown in those years after the first World War when mankind was trying to return slowly to some kind of sanity. Equilibrium, security and orderly entertainment was what men sought as they left their womenfolk at home for their weekly game of football on a Saturday.

Those were not the days of floodlights, but of maxi-skirts and wasp waists for the girls, cloth caps and mufflers for their

1955—CHELSEA'S LEAGUE CHAMPIONSHIP TEAM

Standing: Jack Oxberry (Trainer), Stan Willemse, Ken Armstrong, Peter Sillett, Stan Wicks, Charlie Thomson, Derek Saunders, John Harris. Seated: Eric Parsons, Johnny McNichol, Roy Bentley, Ted Drake (Manager), Seamus O'Connell, Frank Blunstone. Insets (left to right): Ron Greenwood, Bill Robertson, Leslie Stubbs.

beaus, short-back-and-side haircuts, and anyone with a beard had the word 'Beaver!' shouted at him on the street. That was one small expression of social aggression and even that was largely a game: like train-spotting.

Fifty years is a long haul backwards to remember things exactly. For instance, I can't tell you now who were Chelsea's opponents that day I first climbed the high banking which is now covered by the West Stand with its half-a-dozen or so private boxes each costing £650 rental a season.

How strange and far away it all seems now! But I well remember my uncle that day proudly introducing me to 'The Bridge' with a wide, imperious sweep of his hand as if he were unfolding a private empire beneath my young feet. 'And can you see over there,' I seem to recall him saying, 'That weather-vane on top of the main stand on the other side of the ground? It's a footballer. It is George Hilsdon, a famous Chelsea centre-forward who played for England before the war.'

I was impressed. There, Hilsdon stood immortal, the vane spinning N.S.E. and W. above his brow. And as the winds of change have blown across the years, he looked down impassively on that pitch where so many great players have passed and so much has come and gone.

When I first saw Chelsea, Jack Cock was the great presiding figure, another sturdy, honest centre-forward of many goals in an age when shirts were worn outside baggy knee-length shorts; when legs were protected by thick shin-pads and acres of cotton wool; when football boots resembled the footwear worn by the troops in the Flanders mud; and when the ball itself became as heavy as a cannon-ball in bad weather. How those men played at all amazes me now.

Dear Jack Cock, being presented with the Chelsea side to King George V at Stamford Bridge, once made the classic reply to a royal query as they shook hands: 'Yes, sir. Your Majesty has had the honour to meet me before. . . .'

Well, I, too, had the honour: the honour to watch not only Cock but the great cavalcade of players and some of the events that have passed across 'The Bridge'. I even played here once, for Cambridge against Oxford, and thought how lucky I was to use the same dressing-room as some of my heroes of the 1920s—Nils Middelboe, for one, 'the Great Dane', who played for Denmark in the Olympic Games football finals of 1908 and 1912, and who also captained Chelsea as an amateur centre-half for a spell after the first war, later to become a

BACK TO THE TWENTIES . . . AND THIRTIES

Jack Cock
Great, presiding figure as Chelsea's centre-forward, 1919–22, and maker of a classic remark to King George V.

Alec Jackson
Fast as a gazelle, his black hair sleeked back—the Chelsea winger (1930–32) with champagne sparkle in his game.

close friend of mine on his return to Copenhagen. Now well into his 80s, he wrote to me only last season saying that he still looks first at Chelsea's result in the morning paper.

There was Cock, too, of course, whose 21 goals in the 1919–20 season took Chelsea to third place in the First Division; Jack Harrow, upright and spick and span at full-back; Bobby McNeil, a clever ball player at outside-left; Harry Wilding at half-back; and little, fair-haired Tommy Meehan at left-half, busy as a bee and full of honey, who died tragically young.

Though times were hard for many in the 1920s, at least they were fairly leisurely and not so fraught as in the modern world. If wages were lower, so were prices and for 6d. or a bob, one could huddle on the terraces and step into another world to watch the heroic giants of our youth.

The year 1924, however, brought what seemed an insuperable calamity. Chelsea were relegated to the Second Division. My uncle, wore a black tie for a week. Harrow, Wilding, McNeil and Priestley, however, were still wearing their royal blue shirts bravely, and with them there had now come to Stamford Bridge a famous Scottish International inside-left, Andy Wilson. He had been transferred from Middlesbrough who, ironically, also went down with Chelsea that year.

I can still see Wilson in my mind's eye. From 1923 until around 1931, he was the creative spring of the Chelsea attack. Squat of figure, with a withered left hand, padding about the field with short pitter-patter strides that seldom changed pace, he was the ball manipulator who operated in the leisurely gear of that age. Football then and now were different games. There was time to think and space to operate if you were good enough. Teamwork, speed, technique, defensive systems and planning had not reached the pitch of today. The game was more open and individualism enjoyed a freer licence. In many ways it was more fun—certainly less complicated and frenzied—to watch. And Andy Wilson—holding, working the ball close, and

October 1954: Roy Bentley scores at home to West Bromwich and becomes only the second player in Chelsea history to complete a century of League goals for the club. George Mills was the first (1929–39) and two more players have since reached this milestone in marksmanship for Chelsea, Jimmy Greaves and Bobby Tambling. Their individual totals of League goals for the club: Mills 116, Bentley 128, Greaves 124 and Tambling 164.

CHELSEA'S POST-WAR MANAGERS

BILLY BIRRELL, secretary-manager until 1952.
TED DRAKE, Chelsea's first track-suit manager.
TOMMY DOCHERTY—so near to great achievements here.
DAVE SEXTON, thoughtful theorist who has brought Chelsea their biggest honours.

creative—typified his age.

In those years, too, a couple of noted Corinthian amateurs used to turn out for 'The Blues' in their free time. One was A. G. ('Bache') Bower, who gained two full caps for England at full-back; the other, B. Howard Baker, a very fine goalkeeper, also a full England International, who at one time held the British high jump record.

Howard Baker, who was in the paint business, used then to live—and still does, I believe—in the Cheshire area, and it has since been jokingly said that he cost Chelsea more than any professional on the books, what with travelling expenses and the stacks of paint sold to the club by him (drums of the stuff, unused, are said to be still piled up near the railway embankment behind the stand, but it's probably all just a good yarn!)

The year 1930 saw a rebirth. Chelsea won promotion with Blackpool and my uncle became bearable in the house again. There was a resurgence and a new ambition. For years 'The Pensioners' had been a standing music hall joke. The symbol of the club, indeed, lived in the ageing, bent figure dressed in the uniform of an inmate of the Royal Hospital. Kindly, affectionate, but doddering, he was Chelsea to the core. Supported by an easy-going, cosmopolitan community, people used to flock to Stamford Bridge hoping for the best, but expecting the worst and intent in any case on watching the opposition. It was a strange, permissive marriage that somehow survived the worst rocks.

But the 1930s suddenly brought a new ambition. It was as if Chelsea had decided to throw away their hoops and toys and join the big boys. Perhaps the emergence of Arsenal as a super-power on the other side of the city had something to do with it.

Chelsea rolled up their trousers, took off socks and shoes and all at once waded seriously into the transfer market. Almost at one fell swoop they signed Alec Jackson from Huddersfield, Hughie Gallacher, from Newcastle, and Alec Cheyne, from Aberdeen, all Scottish internationals.

If Cheyne was the least well-known of this distinguished trio down south, certainly Gallacher and Jackson needed no introduction. Both members of the renowned Scottish 'Wembley Wizards' of 1928, they were the equivalent Denis Law and George Best of their days. They were colourful, dramatic match-winners in their own right and the crowds flocked to see them.

1970—CHELSEA'S F.A. CUP YEAR
Back row: John Boyle, Eddie McCreadie, Marvin Hinton, Keith Weller, Stewart Houston, Paddy Mulligan. Middle row: Ian Hutchinson, Peter Osgood, Peter Bonetti, David Webb, Tommy Hughes, John Dempsey, Derek Smethurst. Front row: Tommy Baldwin, Charlie Cooke, Ron Harris, Peter Houseman, Alan Hudson, John Hollins.

1971—THE CUP-WINNERS' CUP COMES TO STAMFORD BRIDGE

Standing: Peter Bonetti, Alan Hudson, Peter Feely, Ian Hutchinson, David Webb, John Dempsey, Micky Droy, Derek Smethurst, Stewart Houston, John Boyle, John Hollins, Paddy Mulligan, John Phillips. Seated: Keith Weller, Peter Osgood, Tommy Baldwin, Ron Harris, Peter Houseman, Charlie Cooke, Eddie McCreadie.

Suddenly, with an all-Scottish forward line of Jackson, Cheyne, Gallacher, Wilson and wee Jackie Crawford, Chelsea looked to be in business and capable at last of winning something big. But it all turned out to be a lovely dream. Though Gallacher got 57 goals in his first three seasons and Jackson 25 from the right-wing in a couple, Chelsea seldom rose above half-way in the First Division in that brief excursion.

Yet what a joy it was to watch those men when they were on song. Little Gallacher's tight dribbling and unexpected touches were gossamer at times as he took the breath away with his impish audacity. An artist, his work had all the bloom of water colours.

But for controlled, almost animal, excitement, Alec Jackson was the star of my heaven. I had followed his earlier exploits with Huddersfield Town since the late 1920s, and had watched him try to play Blackburn Rovers on his own in the astonishing Cup Final of 1928 when Huddersfield, one of the hottest odds-on favourites ever, went down at Wembley.

Magnificently built, fast as a gazelle, his black hair sleeked back, he seemed to reach out for the ball as if it were his private property. For 'the Laughing Cavalier', as he was called, there was joy and champagne in his game as he stalked inwards from the wing on the kill, always on the search for an opening with head or foot. Many were the dazzling goals he scored.

Such a favourite was he that I had to share him. So I once took my mother into a 65,000 crowd high on the open west terrace to watch him. Jostled as she was by the swaying mob, and approaching her 60th year, she enjoyed the experience. Jackson scored; I made my point and she shared the excitement of that moment.

In the early '30s, too, there was a fine new full-back partnership in Tommy Law and George Barber whose sliding tackles would give a few referees of today a fit or two. And behind them soon came Vic Woodley, who was to keep goal for England so often.

Another to give esoteric pleasure was Peter O'Dowd, procured from Burnley, who was almost the last of the dying race of attacking centre-halves in an age when the new 'policeman centre-back" had already become a creeping paralysis. Yet with all this galaxy, the prizes still went to Arsenal. Chelsea's eternal role seemed to be that of unpredictable entertainers.

Came the 1950s, the 1960s and now the 70s. Each decade has had its men and moments—Tommy Lawton, Tommy Walker, Roy Bentley and others in their time; momentous F.A. Cup semi-finals against Arsenal, both lost in the end; and one breathtaking 6–5 defeat in the League by Manchester United.

Now the heirs of this long cavalcade have at last broken the ice. Chelsea are no longer the butt of the comedians. The F.A. Cup has been landed, also the European Cup-Winners' Cup; Wembley has been visited again in the League Cup Final. Their eyes and hands are on the prizes in a way that almost shames their predecessors who wilfully, it seemed, at times spurned the material rewards of this life.

If things do not change basically they certainly alter, and Chelsea, in their streamlined modern look, are but part of the revolution of life. Spurred by ambition, hardened, and not softened, by success, they are becoming the urban guerillas. We see the progression through their managers of the last 20 years.

First, Billy Birrell, the gentle, kindly, old-fashioned Scot, who smiled quizzically through thin-rimmed spectacles, an administrator behind a desk rather than a track-suited leader on the pitch.

Next, Ted Drake, who disposed of The Pensioner from the Chelsea programme to change the image of the team once and for all. He succeeded in bringing the League title to Stamford Bridge in 1955 for the first time to celebrate the club's 50th birthday. Yes, Chelsea owe him more than they perhaps realize.

In his steps followed Tommy Docherty, volatile, abrasive, aggressive, a stormy petrel who so nearly reached Everest as he put more fire and mettle in the heels of his men. Today Dave Sexton, the thoughtful theorist, quiet but firm, has brought the revolution its rewards . . . a Chelsea revolution that has now stretched beyond the field to the vast rebuilding operation transforming Stamford Bridge.

The Chelsea of tomorrow may rise even higher than today. The yesterday of long ago and far away, though empty, still retains its romance.

Two £100,000 smiles on September 1, 1971, the day Dave Sexton signed Chris Garland from Bristol City.

The REAL Dave Sexton

By ALAN HOBY *(Sunday Express)*

He has been called deep . . . secretive . . . an enigma . . . a human riddle . . . a manager who, in the endless poker game of football, keeps his mouth buttoned up and his cards close to his chest. A lot of people, in fact, have been fooled by the deadpan public face of Dave Sexton.

Because words—unless carefully thought over beforehand—do not come easily to him . . . because he has an intense dislike of self-advertisement and, when called on to make a speech, conveys the distinct impression that he would rather face a firing squad, many football outsiders have totally misunderstood the ruggedly good-looking 42-year-old Chelsea chief.

All they saw was the 'tip of the iceberg.' They did not see the strength beneath. They did not see the pride, the determination, the courage and character of the man who bosses perhaps the most complex and mercurial squad in the First Division.

Yet the clue which unlocks the personality secrets of David James Sexton—an unusual blend of thinker and man-of-action— is not hard to find. To unearth it you have to go back to the day when Dave's famous boxing father, Archie Sexton, known throughout the profession as 'The Classy Cockney', surprised his son with a sudden unsolicited piece of advice.

'I was just about to join the Army,' Dave Sexton, then a useful amateur welterweight himself, told me, 'and it was the only advice my father ever gave me. "Don't let anyone take the mickey out of you," he said in his quiet way. "Always stick up for yourself." ' The supremo of Stamford Bridge paused, then added significantly: 'In all that I have done since I have tried to act up to that.'

In his fighting prime, round about the jazz-time thirties, Archie Sexton was described by one contemporary critic as

the boxer 'who never quaked or quit.' These qualities whipped the crowd to a frenzy of applause when, in 1933, Sexton senior fought Jock McAvoy, 'The Rochdale Thunderbolt,' for the British middleweight title.

McAvoy, one of the most destructive punchers at his weight the ring has known, stopped the Londoner in the tenth round. But not before the hard-bitten audience had risen to the sportsmanship and bravery under fire of the battered loser.

Later the elder Sexton's career was tragically and prematurely shortened when he lost the sight of one eye. But, until the day he died, he was never heard to complain.

It was this dogged, tenacious streak which Archie passed down to his son . . . the same Sexton who staggered the football world last season when he placed his popular, ball-playing star, Peter Osgood, on the transfer list at a stupefying £250,000—'for not trying.'

The Chelsea clans were stunned. Petititions were signed demanding that Ossie must stay. Some indignant fans even queued all night in protest. But, amid all the anger, what stumped logical minds was how a so-called 'non-trier' could be worth a cold quarter-of-a-million pounds. If Ossie really lacked effort, if he failed to run as much as he should, how on earth—asked the Sexton critics—could he be worth such an enormous sum?

The day Dave came back to The Bridge. The late Charles Pratt, then Chelsea's chairman, welcomes the club's new manager on his appointment in October 1967.

It simply did not make sense. What was Sexton up to? And why, after dropping such a bombshell, did he make such seemingly contradictory statements? What were his motives and why did he wrap them in such mystery?

The answer, of course, lies in Sexton's own ultra-dedicated make-up. Like his father, he is a 100 per center and, at all times, he expects 100 per cent from every single one of his players. Basically, I am sure he had no desire at that time, to sell the controversial Osgood. He merely threatened to . . . because the unpredictable Ossie had not measured up.

In the words of a sympathetic managerial rival: 'Dave did absolutely the right thing. You have got to be a bit of a psychologist in this game. He wanted to give Osgood a jolt. He wanted to jerk him into consistently giving of his best both for Chelsea and for his own future. Sometimes you have to do these things, however unpopular they may make you at the time. That is what separates the good managers from the bad.'

Challenge . . . struggle . . . the ability to overcome setbacks, to master tension and trouble . . . these are the things that fascinate Chelsea's Sexton. They are revealed by his choice of reading. 'I am a great book lover when I get the time. I escape, whenever I can, by reading. I enjoy it. I feel better . . . refreshed. I try to go to bed early two or three times a week so that I can do this. In fact, I would like to have been a writer if football had not claimed me since I was seven.

Wembley 1970: Dave Sexton and Don Revie lead Chelsea and Leeds United into what was to be the first drawn F.A. Cup Final for 58 years . . . and after another epic struggle in the replay at Old Trafford Chelsea won the trophy for the first time.

In good hands! Chairman Brian Mears and Dave Sexton proudly show off the F.A. Cup—and the players who won it—at the civic reception at Fulham Town Hall.

'What particularly interests me is how other people solve *their* problems. I find it helps. It is always fascinating to read about people who have had tremendous pressure and see how they coped. I've read a lot of books on Rommel. He seemed to be a general both sides admired. He was brave in adversity. Even enemies spoke well of him. Another whose work I admire is the American poet, Robert Frost.

'Did you know that he was unrecognised until he was 39? That is a long, long time to go before achieving recognition. The pressures to quit must have been enormous. You need great will-power to keep going without any success until you are nearly 40.'

Sexton also talked of the works of the Jesuit priest, scientist, philosopher and traveller, Pierre Teilhard de Chardin, whose writings were banned by the Vatican until after his death. Chardin, after trouble with his Order, went to America, where he died in 1955.

'What I am trying to say,' said Sexton, 'is that all these people made disappointment work for them. It makes one's own problems seem less Everest-sized.'

But there is nothing pretentious about these outside interests. Sexton is no phoney intellectual—as his musical tastes show. He likes everything, from small-group jazz to the classics; from Errol Garner and Stan Getz to Bach, Beethoven, Sibelius and Mahler. 'I have these cassettes which I listen to in the car.'

At one time he went through a conjuring craze. 'I used to do tricks with pennies and cards. It used to amuse the kids,' he said with a grin. Sexton and his wife Thea have four children, Anne (13), David (12), Michael (6) and Christopher (nearly two).

He broke off, then said reflectively: 'That is one of the troubles with this job. I can't concentrate on their interests half as much as I would like. I don't see them for as long as I should, and often, when I am home on Sundays, I am too tired to take them out. The only time in the whole year we are really together as a family is on our summer holidays. Then I can forget completely about the game.'

But his first passion in life will always be football. 'I am like a Scotsman in this respect,' he told me. 'The Scots really love the game and so do I.'

As a player with Chelmsford, Luton, West Ham, Leyton Orient, Brighton and Crystal Palace Dave Sexton was good but never great. He was an inside-forward with a fierce long-range shot. He could—and did—blast in cannonballs from all angles—to the fear and consternation of opposing goalkeepers.

He is, of course, one of that remarkable West Ham academy of managers and coaches who have spread their intelligence, wit and belief in positive Soccer throughout the League. This illustrious list includes such names as Frank O'Farrell, manager of Manchester United, Malcolm Allison, team manager of Manchester City, Noel Cantwell, formerly

As a West Ham player, Dave Sexton and his team-mates used Phil Cassettari's cafe, just round the corner from Upton Park, for a regular lunch-time football forum. The scene was re-enacted last season, when it became known that the cafe was soon to be demolished. Seated left to right: Jimmy Andrews, Dave Sexton, Noel Cantwell, Malcolm Allison, John Bond, Frank O'Farrell and Malcom Musgrove.

Coventry, George Petchey who now runs Orient, and John Bond, who, in his first season, so successfully took Bournemouth into the Third Division.

'There were a lot of people with a lot of ideas at West Ham then,' says Bond, 'It was around the time (1953) when the Hungarians thrashed England 6–3 at Wembley. I remember Dave coming back after that game humming with excitement and enthusiasm for what he had seen. The Hungarians, led by Puskas, stimulated him, his moods, his ideas, his whole outlook on the game. This was the turning-point for English football. This was the revolution we had all been waiting for.

'We used to meet for lunch at an Italian restaurant in the Barking Road. We talked and talked. We also had many discussions in the club rest-room after practice at Grange Road, West Ham's training ground. You could say it was a melting pot of ideas. Everyone pitched in.

'Dave used to be the chairman at those meetings. People who don't know him tend to believe that he is quiet and reserved. But he can talk on a variety of subjects. He is a most knowledgeable guy.' Bond laughed. 'Although it had nothing to do with football, I remember Dave once announcing in his dry way that he was going to give a talk on cabbages. And he did! He gave a brilliant discourse.

But, in more recent years, light-hearted moments have been brief. Like other top managers, Dave knows that there is no real release from the 'hot seat' of football management. Looking round he sees the ulcers, nervous breakdowns, even the odd heart attack. And deep inside him, like all the others, he realises that he is walking a tightrope.

Outwardly, with his cropped dark hair and fighter's frame, he is the strong-man—the crack coach the Chelsea players asked for when Tommy Docherty left the club in October, 1967. They signed a unanimous 'round robin'. 'Sexton can put us right up there with the others,' said skipper Ron Harris.

Outwardly, he is the track-suited tactician who, in two sky-high seasons, lifted Chelsea to epic triumphs in the F.A. Cup and European Cup-Winners' Cup. Last season he also guided them to the League Cup Final at Wembley.

Outwardly, he is the manager who, three years ago, led the successful charge of the then 'soft South'—Don Revie's scathing words—against the arrogant domination of the North. Remember the rejoicing, the almighty booze-up down the King's Road when Chelsea, after grimly hanging on to force a 2–2 draw against a super Leeds side in the F.A. Cup

That's a lot of whisky for a man who doesn't drink! Taking Chelsea to last season's League Cup Final earned Dave the Bell's Scotch Whisky award for January 1972—a £100 cheque and the gallon bottle presented here by Tony Derry, the company's U.K. sales manager.

Final at Wembley, fantastically won the replay 2–1 at Old Trafford?

Remember, too, the chortling, chanting coveys of Chelsea fans in Athens, wildly brandishing Union Jacks after the Blues had whipped Real Madrid in another replayed Final? Who will ever forget it, or the quite spontaneous, highly emotional rendering of 'For He's A Jolly Good Fellow' by the whole Chelsea team as they toasted 'The Boss' in champagne after the game?

This is the man who six days a week throughout the long, gruelling grind of the season gets up at 7a.m. and commutes from his Hove home to Stamford Bridge, S.W.6. It is a regular routine—a clockwork schedule, snow or shine, damp or dry.

Ninety-nine times out of a hundred he will stick up for his squad with protective loyalty and I pity the man foolish enough to criticise any Chelsea player to his face. And this is what I like about him. When he has to dress down one of his footballers, normally, he does it in private, eyeball to eyeball.

It is only when his exasperation, his frustration at any particular player's lack of total application stretches his patience to breaking point that, at last, he explodes like some long-delayed time bomb.

That is Dave Sexton . . . a manager with a mission . . . a boss who, somehow, despite Chelsea's exasperating slip-ups in games they should never have lost—such as against Atvidaberg, the Swedish part-timers, last season and then Orient from a position of two up in the F.A. Cup—still believes in their tremendous talent. His biggest problem, as I see it, is how to graft consistency onto their obvious class; how to weld their disparate temperaments into a Championship,

as well as a cup-fighting, force. It is just one more case of 'making disappointment work for you.'

Winning . . . winning attractively and well . . . that is what matters. After most Saturday home games he walks from Stamford Bridge to Victoria to catch the train home. He smiled, then added: 'It is quite a long walk, but I enjoy it. It helps me to relax. Of course, the walk is much more pleasant if we have won . . .'

You won't find two more dedicated managers than Dave Sexton and Liverpool's Bill Shankly. But there are times when even they are beaten—on this occasion by the weather. It was February 1970 when this snow-covered Stamford Bridge pitch gave them what none of us likes . . . a Saturday afternoon without football.

Dick Spence: 38 years at Stamford Bridge

Dick Spence put ten crisp pound notes in his pocket on the day he arrived at Stamford Bridge. That was in October 1934, when five-figure signing-on fees were undreamed of. But Dick was well satisfied. He had never seen that sort of money in the Yorkshire pits, or at Barnsley, who collected a £5,000 fee for the 22-year-old right-winger.

Now, 38 years later, he is easily the longest-serving member of the Chelsea staff. His playing career here lasted 14 years, and the 19 League goals he scored in his first season still stand as a record for a Chelsea winger.

When he stopped playing in 1948 after breaking his right leg in a London Challenge Cup match against Tottenham, he was given a backroom job, first as third team trainer and after the 'A' side was disbanded helping, in turn, Dick Foss, Frank Blunstone and now Ken Shellito in the Youth section.

He still believes in teaching by example. He often joins in five-a-side games with Chelsea's boy players and chuckles 'I can run as fast as any of them.'

On Saturday afternoons Dick helps first-team trainer Harry Medhurst with the dressing-room duties, and his cheerful presence lifts a lot of the tightness from the keyed-up players. He refuses even to think about retirement. 'I'll carry on for as long as Chelsea need me,' he says.

Soccer did not become his life until he was in his twenties. He was one of six children, his father was out of work and he had to make a contribution to the family budget. Football seemed too precarious, so like thousands of other 14-year-olds in the mining villages of Yorkshire, young Spence went down the pit when he left school.

He began as a pony driver earning 2s.5d a day. 'You couldn't buy a job in the mines in those days, so I had to hang on to it,' he recalls. 'If I'd gone in for football first and not made the grade, I'd have been pushed to find work.

'I handed over all my wages except three shillings for spending money. Once a fortnight I used to lash out two bob on fixed-odds betting. If my five homes came up I could afford to go the the pictures. If not, I had a game of football.'

Spence also added to his earning when sprint races were held at the summer fairs. He would pay a shilling to enter the handicap, and often dashed home first to win the 50-shilling prize.

Meanwhile, he was playing regularly for a colliery side, as an inside-forward. Brough Fletcher, then Barnsley's manager, showed interest, but Dick was reluctant to turn professional. He was 5ft.5¼in and under nine stone, and doubted whether he was big enough or good enough for League football.

'Fletcher was a grand bloke, but I turned him down three times before I finally agreed to a trial in the Midland League. After three games he told me the directors had decided that if Barnsley beat Norwich that Saturday and got into the next round of the Cup, they could afford to sign me.

Dick Spence in Chelsea colours soon after his £5,000 transfer from Barnsley in October 1934. He has served under five managers at Stamford Bridge: Leslie Knighton, Billy Birrell, Ted Drake, Tommy Docherty and Dave Sexton.

'They beat Norwich easily at Oakwell, so I signed on the following Thursday and played against Hartlepools two days later. I scored in the first five minutes, and that set me on the right road.' Almost overnight, from working in dimly-lighted coal-mines, Dick found himself playing in football's fierce spotlight.

That game was the start of Spence's career as a winger. Fletcher insisted he played there, despite protests. The manager was quickly proved right, and Dick admits: 'He was a shrewd man.'

He stayed for little more than a season, during which he helped Barnsley to win the Third Division (North) Championship. He scored 13 goals, and one of them—at New Brighton—clinched promotion.

That form made Spence the target of three clubs—Grimsby Town, Manchester City and Chelsea. Dick didn't know what to do. Finally, he decided to talk with each manager. 'First I saw the Grimsby boss, then the Manchester City manager. They didn't impress me.

'Mr. Leslie Knighton, manager of Chelsea, put £10 on the table. He asked me whether I would like to go to London. At that time I had hardly been to the seaside, let alone London. He said that if I signed, the money would be mine. I asked him for a pen, and signed there and then.'

Dick's starting wages with Chelsea were £8 a week in the season and £6 in the summer . . . a big rise, because at Barnsley his pay was £3.5s when in the team and £2.10s if he wasn't. He was single then, and he moved into digs in Fulham Road.

The biggest problem caused by his move seemed to be the London bread. 'My mother used to make her own, and I couldn't get on at first with bakers' loaves. They stuck on my chest, and caused indigestion.'

The match with Arsenal in October 1935 stands out of a host of memories. That day the official Chelsea crowd record of 82,905 was set up, and spectators spilled over on to the dog track. As he sped down the wing, Spence wondered whether he would trip over the fans.

It was one of his finest games, but he remembers it also for a remarkable goal scored by Arsenal's left-winger Cliff Bastin. 'Cliff shot from just inside our half, and he hit the ball so hard that goalkeeper Vic Woodley didn't even move.' The result: Chelsea 1 Arsenal 1.

Spence scored an equally great goal in a 1–1 draw at Highbury. Picking up the ball in his own half, he went past

Wilf Copping, beat a full-back and drew the goalkeeper before shooting past him. Alex James, who was reporting the game for a newspaper, wrote that it was one of the finest goals he had seen.

Spence has other vivid recollections . . . like getting all four when Liverpool were beaten 4–1 at The Bridge in his first season here, and scoring a hat-trick in a 3–2 defeat of Preston, also at home.

Now that the orthodox winger is seldom seen, it is fascinating to hear Spence talk about his role. Chelsea decided to build him up physically, but had little success. At 5ft.5¼in he has never weighed more than ten stone despite a ration of Guinness. 'I couldn't stand the stuff then, but now I never drink anything else.'

Spence's exceptional speed more than compensated for his lack of weight, and it gave him a great advantage over the cumbersome full-backs of the thirties and forties.

'In those days there was man-to-man marking, and most full-backs were built like tanks. I was lucky, because I could go both ways, but the left-backs were invariably left-footers. Two or three times I would go down the line against an opponent, then suddenly I would switch and cut across on to his "dummy" side. Once I knew his weak spot, I would work on it.'

Spence's inside partners included Jimmy Argue, the strong Scot. Behind him was Irishman Billy Mitchell, who was nicknamed 'the wire man'. Listen to Dick describing a typical Chelsea attack: 'When the ball was played down our left wing, the defence would move across. I kept wide out on the right.

'When the ball came over I would be making a blind-side dash to the post. If my timing was right, I arrived at the same time as the ball, and I could flick it in with my head. A lot of my goals came that way.'

Spence had a hard shot as well, and he attributes this to his

When a broken leg ended Dick's playing career in 1948, he joined the Stamford Bridge backroom staff. He became third team trainer and, after that side was disbanded, switched to Chelsea's Youth team. Left to right in this Chelsea picture from the middle 1950s: Albert Tennant (coach), Harry Medhurst (assistant-trainer), Dick Spence ('A' team trainer), Jack Oxberry (first-team trainer) and Ted Drake (manager).

years down the mine. Bent over in the cramped conditions, he had to use his leg muscles to propel loaded trucks along the tracks. He reckons this work made him as strong as a player two stones heavier.

The statistics of his playing career are impressive. He made 221 First Division appearances for Chelsea and scored 62 goals. He also won two England caps, against Austria and Belgium on the 1936 summer tour. There might have been further international recognition had it not been for the emergence of young Stanley Matthews. Spence twice finished on the losing side in a team disrupted by injury.

'We had only been playing Austria in Vienna for a quarter of an hour when Ray Bowden of Arsenal damaged a cartilage and had to go off. There were no substitutes in those days, so we had to play on with ten men and were beaten 2–1. Three days later against Belgium in Brussels, Middlesbrough's George Camsell broke his nose and needed stitches in his face. We were back to ten men again, and we lost that one as well, 3–2. I thought I played well, but that was it as far as England was concerned. Matthews came along soon after.'

Following war service in the Army, Dick resumed his career in 1946. He was asked to strengthen the reserves in a Combination Cup game at Tottenham and he broke his right leg.

'All told I played only about three reserve games for Chelsea,' he recalls. 'But I agreed to miss a first-team tour to help out at Tottenham. I was out for the rest of the season, and manager Billy Birrell asked me if I would like to come on the coaching staff.

Running repairs on the field (left) and off (centre) from Dick Spence, a Chelsea star of yesterday, for perhaps some stars of tomorrow.

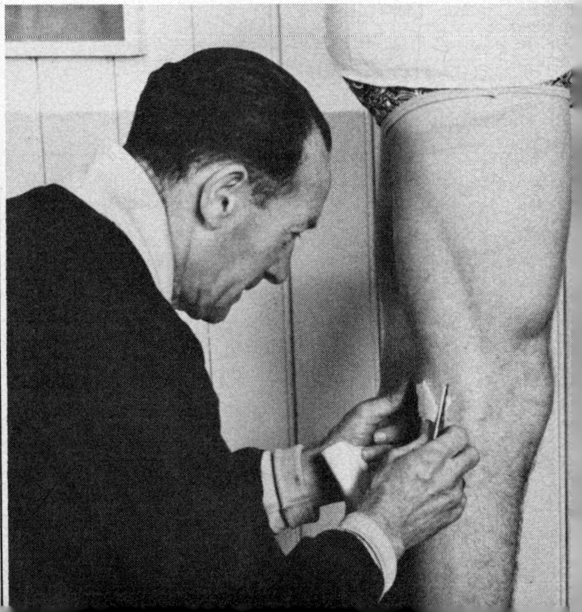

Put me among the boys! Dick Spence is still as happy-go-lucky, as enthusiastic for Chelsea as the day he arrived at Stamford Bridge in 1934. 'Working among young people helps to keep you young,' he says . . . and if there's half a chance he'll join them in five-a-sides.

'It was a bit of a shock, but I realised I wouldn't get any better as a player, and I decided to accept.'

Spence took courses in physiotherapy and coaching to equip himself for his new career. He began as "A" team trainer, then switched to the Youth section.

He looks back with pleasure on some of the Chelsea players he has seen come up from boys. 'I must rate Jimmy Greaves as the greatest natural player I have seen, although Peter Osgood runs him close. Both cost Chelsea nothing. There have been many others, among them Terry Venables, Barry Bridges and Peter Bonetti.'

Nobody can be better qualified than Dick Spence to select Chelsea's greatest players down the years. Either he has played alongside them, watched them develop from the junior ranks or as new signings from other clubs. It's a task which he approaches with a great deal of thought, and he says it's just impossible to choose between some.

The goalkeeper in Dick's best all-time Chelsea XI is Peter Bonetti. 'I pick Peter even though Vic Woodley got a stack of caps. My right-back is Ken Shellito, who was starting to be a great player when injury ended his career, and his partner is Eddie McCreadie, whose speed gets him the vote over big Welshman Bill Hughes.

'If I wanted an attacking right-half, he would be John Hollins. Ken Armstrong would come in if a defensive job was needed. John Harris is centre-half . . . he was a natural. So was Sam Weaver, my choice at left-half.

'I would have Peter Brabrook on the right-wing, because Charlie Cooke is really a midfield man. Greaves is number eight, and then I come to a problem—who to choose between Roy Bentley and Tommy Lawton for centre-forward?

'Alan Hudson is going to be one of the best, so he comes in at inside-left. Frank Blunstone is my left-winger. He was a great club man and always a 100 per cent trier.'

Modestly Spence does not press his own claims, but over the years he thrilled thousands with his wing play—and it's a safe bet that they would vote him into the elite company. Dick has never been a lover of the high life. He enjoys a game of snooker and a flutter on the horses, and another of his loves is cricket—he still plays for Northolt's Sunday side.

Chelsea is still his life—and even after 38 years, he is as enthusiastic as the newest boy to join the juniors.

Two of his best stories he tells with a laugh, at his own expense—literally. Somehow, Barnsley never got round to paying him his accrued share of benefit from his long-ago transfer to Chelsea. Says Dick: 'For years after, whenever I saw their Chairman, Joe Richards, I'd say "How about my accrued share, Mr. Richards?" and he'd give me a wink and a smile and say he'd see what could be done. It never came, and it won't now . . . but I've had my moneysworth in smiles about it.'

As a sporting man ever-loyal to Chelsea, Dick felt it his duty to back them every January, before the third round, to win the F.A. Cup. Year in and year out, he placed his bet at odds of 25–1 and sometimes as high as fifties. There were near-misses in the semi-finals of 1950 and 1952 and in the Final of 1967, but never a touch. So at last Dick gave up his annual Cup flutter. That was in 1970 . . . . the year Chelsea won the Cup!

Oh, the Questions You Ask Chelsea

You write . . . you telephone . . . you cable . . . you call . . . and over the years all the questions Chelsea have been asked by their fans would fill not this chapter but a whole encyclopaedia. Few sporting bodies attract from the public queries and enquiries right through the calendar like the top-level football club. It is all part of the business, and the day Chelsea's telephone stops ringing, when the postman finds no reason to call and there's no one to be served at the ticket-office window is the day when they can really start to worry.

Chelsea's switchboard is never quiet. Match-days it is jammed with callers ringing during and after the game to find out what's the score and who got the goals. During the week, ticket enquiries alone comprise one whole aspect of club life, with the volume growing round by round when Cup-ties come along.

In modern times questioners of a new type have arrived on the scene—girl fans asking for players' telephone numbers and addresses (they don't get them!) and whether particular players are married or single . . . which of them have fan clubs, etc. Autograph requests form a big percentage of the club post-bag.

A new player who suddenly captures the crowd's imagination becomes a fresh subject for questions, such as Chris Garland was last season. It wasn't long before they were asking such things as 'Is he naturally left- or right-footed?' and 'What are his ambitions with Chelsea?', to which Chris was happy to reply: 'I'm naturally right-footed, and as far as the future is concerned my ambition is to establish myself in the First Division. Chelsea did terrific things in the two seasons before I came. The future can be even greater for the club, and I want to play my part in it.'

(*Opposite, above*) No doubt about the question Chelsea fans asked most last season: When will Ian Hutchinson be ready to play again? Up in the Stamford Bridge physiotherapy room Harry Medhurst removes the specially-designed second plaster that was fitted to help Ian's recovery from that broken leg.

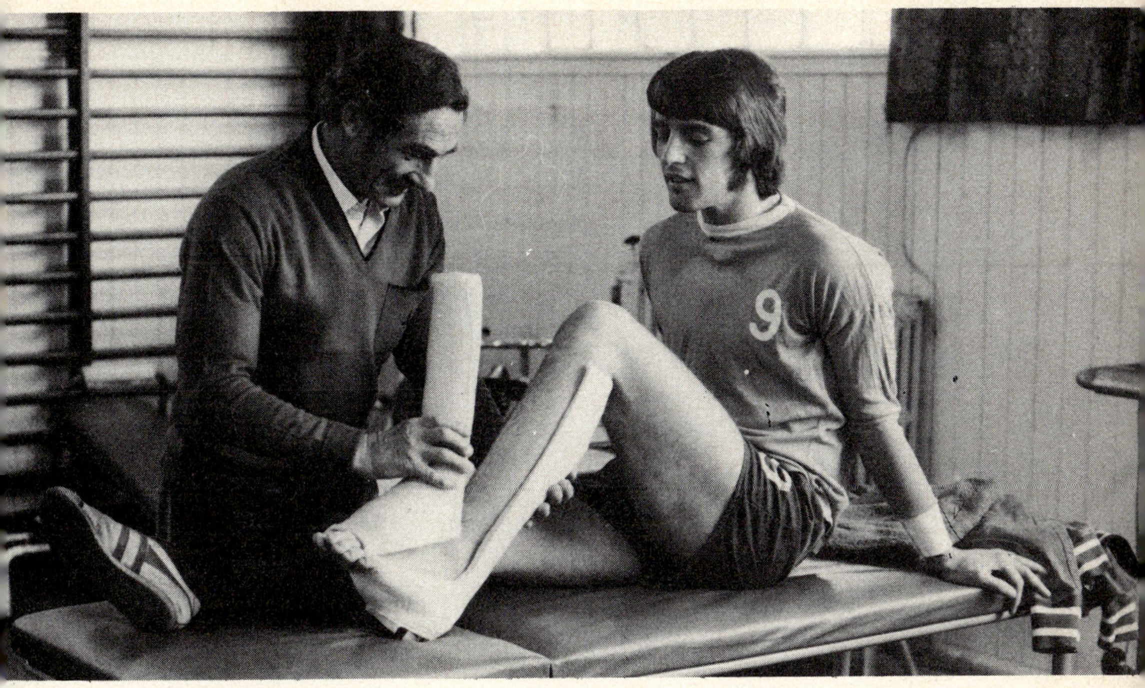

(Below) Chris Garland makes a 'lucky draw' for the Chelsea Pool on the day he was signed from Bristol City. With him is Pools Organiser Geoff Abel. In its first two years, Chelsea's became the third largest club pool in the Football League and contributed £72,000 towards the ambitious redevelopment programme now in progress at Stamford Bridge.

Last winter's most-asked question was: How is Ian Hutchinson getting on . . . when will he be playing again? After his cartilage operation on the right knee in April 1971 and the broken left leg sustained the following August, let's hope the answer is pleasing to everyone, most of all to Ian, this season.

For several years supporters have kept up a steady bombardment of questions about ground improvements at Stamford Bridge. At last, they're getting the sort of answer they've waited so patiently for. Another well-worn query—thoroughly justified in its constant repetition, it has to be admitted—was: What is being done to improve Chelsea's loudspeaker system, which must be among the least audible in the Football League? Last season's answer was the same as it had been for as long as one can remember—that 'steps were being taken' to improve it. Roll on, new stadium and the promised new public address system which, we are assured, WILL work to general satisfaction.

Over the years Chelsea have been asked thousands of times to identify the footballer-figure which adorned the weather-vane on top of the East Stand. It depicted a long-ago striker named George Hilsdon, first player to score a century of first-team goals for the club. And a macabre note has been struck, too, by many a widow asking if 'my late husband's ashes might be scattered over the pitch, as he was such a devoted fan of Chelsea all through his life?' The sentiment is appreciated, the request politely declined.

Yes, all the time, all sorts of people ask all sorts of questions about Chelsea. It may lighten the postman's load a little . . . quieten the switchboard for just a few moments of the day to set out some of them here, though for space reasons this is to mention but a fraction of the most-raised queries.

Who was Chelsea's biggest-ever player, physically speaking?

Our first goalkeeper, Bill ('Little Willie') Foulke, who stood 6ft. 2in., weighed 22st. at the time he played for us in season 1905–06 . . . and wore size 24 collars!

What is the official attendance record for Stamford Bridge?

82,905 when Chelsea and Arsenal drew 1–1 in the First Division on October 12, 1935, Receipts were £4,698 10s. (in those days of one-shilling admission football practically gave itself away). When Chelsea played Moscow Dynamo here on November 13, 1945, the crowd was estimated at approaching 100,000, but some 20,000 of them broke in without paying and the officially announced attendance that day was 74,496.

Which player has won most full International honours (any country) during his service to Chelsea?

Eddie McCreadie, who has played 23 times for Scotland. Take a bow, Eddie . . . and a bumper Testimonial this season!

Was it a record when Chelsea played a different goalkeeper in four successive first-team matches last season—Peter Bonetti at Coventry (December 17), John Phillips v. Tottenham in League Cup semi-final first leg (December 22), David Webb v. Ipswich (December 27) and Steve Sherwood at Derby (January 1)?

Certainly a Chelsea record . . . and, as far as we know, a record for any League club, too.

Going back to pre-war football, did Chelsea's two International goalkeepers Vic Woodley and Johnny Jackson—who were on the club's books at the same time—ever face each other in a full International between England and Scotland?

No, they did not. While he was with Chelsea, Johnny Jackson played for Scotland against England twice, in 1934 and 1935; Vic Woodley was England's goalkeeper against Scotland in three International Championships—1937, 1938 and 1939.

Which of Chelsea's present players have official fan clubs?

Three at the time of going to press: Peter Osgood, David Webb and Alan Hudson.

How much money has the Chelsea Pools Association raised towards the redevelopment of Stamford Bridge?

At the end of last season, after two years in operation, the profits of the Chelsea Pools (including Golden Goals) totalled £72,000—all of it helping to pay for the mammoth redevelopment of the stadium.

In Chelsea's history, has the average home League attendance for a complete season ever reached 50,000?

Not quite—the record is 48,350 in 1954–55, our Championship-winning season, when home League crowds topped a million for the first time. Twelve First Division gates at Stamford Bridge that season exceeded 50,000, with the biggest attendance 75,043 against Wolves on Easter Saturday.

Why are they the Goodies? 'Because', said their spokesman, Dave Sexton, 'we never argue in our practice matches . . . never cause trouble . . . pick up the opposition when we knock them down . . . always accept the referee's decision—because I'm the referee!' Back row Goodies: David Webb, Paddy Mulligan, Dave Sexton, Charlie Cooke, Steve Kember. Front row Goodies: Alan Hudson, Ron Suart, Tommy Baldwin, Chris Garland.

What is Chelsea's official nickname—are they still The Pensioners or is it The Blues?

Ted Drake dropped the Pensioner as the club emblem when he became manager in 1952 and officially we have since been The Blues. But habit dies hard, and a lot of older supporters still know us as The Pensioners.

Is it true that gold is hidden under the West Stand?

Yes, real gold! But you can put away your picks and shovels—it's buried at a depth of 30ft. or more, and has been there since the early part of the century, when the popular side terracing was under construction. It was built on tons and tons of clay which had been dumped there during the

And who are the Baddies? Fists raised and teeth clenched, they are strong and clever and good arguers and beat the Chelsea Goodies nearly every time. (And if you believe all this, you'll believe anything!) Back row Baddies: Peter Houseman, Marvin Hinton, John Dempsey, John Boyle, Ron Harris, John Phillips. Front row Baddies: John Hollins, Peter Bonetti, Peter Osgood, Eddie McCreadie.

construction of the Piccadilly Tube. Also tipped into the hardcore were the remains of the Georgian mansion of Lord Phillimore, which was then being demolished by Messrs. Mears, contractors. Driving a pick into a plaster wall, a workman released a cascade of hidden coins. He kept one as a souvenir, and by the time it had been identified as a valuable spade guinea, the rest of the small fortune was buried deep in the rubble at Stamford Bridge.

Was it a record for a Chelsea player other than a forward when John Hollins scored in six consecutive matches (League, League Cup and Cup-Winners' Cup) last August–September?

Yes it was . . . and in answer to the follow-up question as to

Question: Which Cup have Chelsea held unchallenged for 27 years? This is it—the London Football (or League South) War Cup, which was won by Reading in 1941, Brentford in 1942, Arsenal in 1943, Charlton in 1944 and Chelsea in 1945. With the F.A. Cup competition resumed in season 1945–46, the War Cup was never contested again. Hence its permanent place at Stamford Bridge.

Eddie McCreadie, who has won more International honours than anyone else while in the service of Chelsea, takes a well-earned Testimonial this season.

who holds the scoring sequence record by a Chelsea forward, it is Roy Bentley, who netted in eight consecutive matches (seven ones and a two) in September—October 1952. Other good scoring sequences by Chelsea forwards: Jimmy Greaves got a 'single' in six successive games in January–February 1959, and in October–November 1962 Bobby Tambling scored 12 goals (2, 3, 1, 2, 2, 2) in six successive Second Division games.

Is it true that Chelsea sell match programmes to an average of more than 80 per cent of the spectators who come to Stamford Bridge?

Yes, and at some matches the sales percentage has gone above ninety. At all first-team home games last season (1971–72) we sold a grand total of 917,249 programmes, average 87 per cent of spectators. Chelsea's record programme-sale was 1,072,707 (30 matches) in season 1970–71.

And here's a flashback to April 7, 1945, the day Chelsea won this trophy—still their only victory at Wembley. King George VI presents the Cup to John Harris (who was still officially a war-time guest player on loan from Wolves) after the 2–0 victory over Millwall.

Who is the youngest player to appear for Chelsea in competitive first-team football?

Ian (Chico) Hamilton, who was 16 years, 4 months, 18 days old when he made his League debut and scored in the 1–1 draw at Tottenham on March 18, 1967. He subsequently joined Southend and is now with Aston Villa.

What are the highest transfer fees Chelsea have paid and received for players?

Highest fee paid: £170,000 for Steve Kember, from Crystal Palace, in September 1971. Highest fees received: £100,000 for Alan Birchenall, who moved to Crystal Palace in June 1970, and for Keith Weller, transferred to Leicester City in September 1971.

Which came first to Stamford Bridge—floodlights or the West Stand?

Floodlight football was introduced here in March 1957. The West Stand was first used in season 1965–66.

Why are Chelsea's terrace fans so often left out when it comes to buying special Cup-tie tickets? Season-ticket holders always get first priority, but equally loyal terrace supporters don't get a look in—surely there must be a better way of allocating these tickets?

Season-ticket holders deserve some priority; after all, they take a chance on getting a good season's football when they put down a year's money in advance (terrace fans can, and often do, stay away if things don't turn out successfully on the field). In any case, regular standing supporters do have every chance of qualifying for a Cup Final ticket under our programme-voucher system, which worked extremely well when we got to Wembley in 1967, 1970 and 1972. Note: During the present rebuilding of Stamford Bridge, it seems probable (at the time of writing) that even season-ticket holders will have to ballot for tickets at home Cup-ties. The reason is that some of the seats they occupy at League matches will be required to make up the compulsory allocation of 25 per cent of all seating to which visiting clubs are entitled at F.A. Cup matches.

And, in conclusion, the question Stamford Bridge fans have been asking in the early stages of every season since the club was formed: How are Chelsea going to do *this* season?

For the answer we must wait, with fingers crossed, in hope of further dreams of playing success coming true next Spring. That is when the prizes are handed out . . . but Championships are won every bit as much in the opening weeks and middle months as in the grand finale of April and May.

The Stars who follow Chelsea

For years now, autograph-hunters have had a double chance on match days at Stamford Bridge. It isn't only the players' signatures they can collect but, up in the stands, there is always the prospect of 'capturing' some of the biggest names in the world of Entertainment.

At the top, of course, we have **Richard Attenborough**, a director of Chelsea Football Club. His election to the Board in November 1969 showed that even at a club of Chelsea's eminence it is possible to rise in stature from terrace fan—which he was from the early war years—to board-room administrator. There's democracy for you!

As London's West End team, and with big-name players traditionally providing entertainment of a high level ever since the club was formed, it is natural that Chelsea should appeal to so many football-minded personalities in show business. Dance orchestra leader **Victor Silvester** is the doyen of them all in his long-standing (and, in what now seems the distant past, long-suffering) devotion to Chelsea. He says: 'I've been a supporter since I was a boy and a season-ticket holder since I could afford one. Working pre-war in the West End meant that Stamford Bridge was within easy reach, and once I became attached to Chelsea, I was hooked and have been ever since. Back in the thirties, we Chelsea supporters were happy to win matches . . . never dreamed of winning cups. Entertainers like Hughie Gallacher, Alec Jackson and others compensated for the honours that never came the club's way. Today, it's a different world . . . a different Chelsea. The fascination is just as great, and the modern Chelsea are capable of winning the game's top prizes. As far as possible, I keep Saturdays free from professional engagements, because that's my football day . . . my Chelsea day.'

(*Left*) VICTOR SILVESTER, doyen of Chelsea's showbiz supporters.

(*Right*) ARTHUR ASKEY, an ardent supporter of The Blues.

Did you know that Roy Bentley, one of the all-time great Chelsea goalscorers, came to Stamford Bridge on the recommendation of **George Elrick**, the disc-jockey who compered 'Housewives' Choice' on BBC radio for 21 years and is now an artistes' manager who still does compering, cabaret and after-dinner entertaining? Recalls George: 'I was playing the Newcastle Empire just after the war and looked in one Saturday at St. James's Park. It was only a reserve game, but I was absolutely knocked out by the form of their centre-forward. He had class all over him, terrific heading ability, and I just couldn't make out what he was doing in the 'stiffs'. So I got in touch with my good friend Billy Birrell, then manager of Chelsea . . . and six weeks later Roy Bentley moved from Newcastle to Stamford Bridge. Of course, Billy may have had tabs on him already, but I always like to think that the day I looked in at Newcastle Reserves had something to do with Roy coming to Chelsea.'

George, who hails from Aberdeen, was lured to Chelsea by his wife, Alice. 'She's a Chelsea girl . . . her family were all Chelsea fans. I had to join them or I wouldn't have got the girl! Part of the fascination for me has been the Scots here down the years—such as Billy Birrell, Tommy Walker, John

Harris (he's still a great personal friend) right up to the players of the seventies like Charlie Cooke and Eddie McCreadie.'

As a lad up on Merseyside, **Arthur Askey** used to watch Everton. 'They were The Blues, so it followed that when I came to London to work, I should take a fancy to The Blues at Stamford Bridge.' When the weather is fine, Arthur likes to walk from his Kensington luxury flat to take his Saturday afternoon breath of fresh air watching Chelsea, but he admits to having 'another' team—West Ham. Says Arthur: 'There's a friendly feeling about both boardrooms that you don't find everywhere.'

Michael Crawford, five years a Stamford Bridge spectator and a particular pal of David Webb, was unable to join in the applause for any late goals Chelsea scored last season. He had to leave every Saturday home game a few minutes before the end and dash to the matinee performance of the comedy 'No Sex Please. We're British' at The Strand Theatre. Michael admits to getting 'heavily involved' when watching Chelsea: 'One minute I'm shouting "Up the Blues" and the next I'm yelling "Rubbish!" at the opposition. And if anyone near me has a go at a Chelsea player, I have a go back. I wouldn't miss even a bad game. I learn something from 'em all . . . about football and people.'

For 25 years **Sydney Tafler** used to go racing most Saturdays—at the track or 'on the box'. His son Jonathan, then ten, changed all that some three years ago. Sydney explains: 'For weeks he kept on at me to go to Chelsea with him and one day, just for a bit of peace and quiet, I decided to give the horses a miss. By the time I came home from Stamford Bridge that night, I was hooked. Now we're a Chelsea-mad family. I reckon what I've saved on the horses has paid for our season-tickets.'

An injury received when playing football for a Showbiz team led to comedian **Mike Winters** becoming a Chelsea fanatic. 'It happened about eight years ago,' says Mike. 'I was invited along to Stamford Bridge to get some treatment, and trainer Harry Medhurst soon put me right. From that time I've been a Chelsea man—but I still can't make my brother Bernie see sense. He's nuts about Arsenal!'

Bill Oddie—he's the short, stocky one in The Goodies TV series—put Chelsea 'on approval' in 1965 when business brought him to London, and has been a season-ticket holder ever since. Says Bill: 'I come to be entertained, to enjoy the

JUDY GEESON, Chelsea's 'Girl Next Door'.

THE CRAWFORDS are two of Chelsea's most enthusiastic fans. If MICHAEL has to miss a game because of theatre commitments, he can count on his wife, GABRIELLE, to give him a first-hand account.

superb skills of players like Peter Osgood, Alan Hudson and such. Never mind what some of the coaches have done to the game, entertainment is what it's all about. My ideal match, every Saturday right through the season, would be Chelsea versus Manchester United.'

Edinburgh-born **Ronnie Corbett** grew up as a Heart of Midlothian supporter and graduated up there on the supreme skills of Tommy Walker after the 'Ace of Hearts' had returned to Tynecastle from Chelsea. Ronnie has been coming to Stamford Bridge since Tommy Docherty was manager here, and divides his soccer watching in London between Chelsea and Crystal Palace, the club nearest his home.

If Chelsea should decide to install high stools in their new East Stand for little 'fun men' like Arthur Askey and Ronnie Corbett, they'll need a third for **Charlie Drake.** As a boy he watched Millwall, but while his stage career was developing Charlie found little time for football. He came back to it at

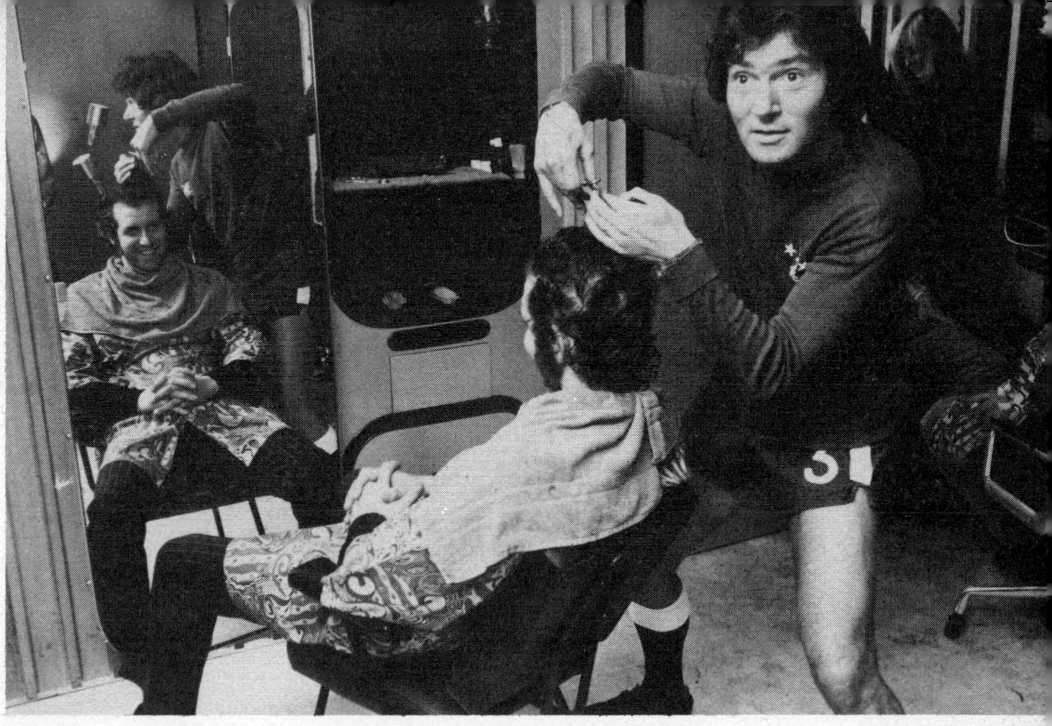

West End hair stylist VIDAL SASSOON, loyally dressed in the Chelsea playing strip, gets to work on the hair of Peter Osgood before last season's League Cup Final.

Chelsea, brought here by a friend who had a spare season-ticket. Charlie sees continued success on the Stamford Bridge sky-line and forecasts: 'With so much talent on tap here, I'm sure we'll be making a big noise about Chelsea again this season, like we did in 1970 and 1971.'

Sam Kydd, rugged-featured star of TV, theatre, films and radio, has been coming regularly to Stamford Bridge for 25 years and a season-ticket holder since 1952. What first attracted him here when, as a boy, he moved with his family from Belfast to Shepherds Bush? Replies Sam: 'It was Chelsea's pre-war Irish Internationals, Tom Priestley and Joe Bambrick. Real heroes they were to me. In those days it was sixpence for us kids to get in. At times when the ground was packed tight, I'd pretend to faint and get passed over the heads from the back of the crowd to the front. Terrific, a view like that for a tanner!'

Another showbiz star who has been coming to Stamford Bridge since he was a boy—except when working abroad— is **Lance Percival**.

So has **Vidal Sassoon**, who was born at Shepherds Bush,

CHARLIE DRAKE—'We'll be making a big noise about Chelsea again this season', is his forecast for 1972–73.

RODNEY BEWES is still very much a 'Likely Lad'—likely to be found at Stamford Bridge on match-days.

grew up in London's East End and has climbed the ladder from shampoo-boy to become one of the world's leading hair stylists. He divides his time between London and New York, and made a point of flying back from America to give Chelsea's players and their wives a special hair-do for the League Cup Final last March. Vidal first came to the Bridge in the days when Tommy Lawton, of the shining black hair and sharp, centre parting, was heading and shooting great goals as Chelsea's centre-forward just after the war. Nowadays, when Stateside of the Atlantic, Mr. Sassoon steps out from his home on New York's East 62nd Street to a Times Square news-stand late on Saturday nights to buy the first paper that carries the day's English football results. He cannot wait a minute longer than is necessary to find out how Chelsea have got on. Vidal Sassoon has brought showmanship to hairdressing, and welcomes Chelsea's big redevelopment plans as long overdue: 'Let's face it, Stamford Bridge has been behind the times as a stadium for as long as I can remember . . . for as long as probably anyone can remember. At last the club is aware that

BILL GAUNT knows how to beat the parking problems round Stamford Bridge on Saturday afternoon. He comes by bike!

RONNIE CORBETT grew up in Edinburgh on the skills of former Chelsea ace Tommy Walker.

the modern spectator needs modern facilities, and I'm delighted.'

Star of another sport and one of Chelsea's most ardent fans is **Jim Laker**, former England cricketer and now BBC cricket commentator. He likes to watch The Blues from behind the North End goal, with his 18-year-old daughter Angela. The Laker family live nearby at Putney, and Jim says: 'I'd rather have twenty minutes of Chelsea with the skills of Alan Hudson and Peter Osgood than watch England for a whole match. For the customer, football is all about entertainment.'

Impresario **Harold Davison**, executive director of the 'Tom Jones and Englebert Humperdinck Company,' Management, Agency & Music, once brought Frank Sinatra to share his West Stand box. . . and a few weeks later Frank rang him from Palm Springs at midnight to ask how Chelsea had got on that afternoon.

Dance-band leader **Sydney Thompson** and his wife Mary come to Stamford Bridge in all weathers and regardless of whom Chelsea are playing. 'We hate to miss any match, friendlies, testimonials, anything,' says Sydney. 'As real supporters we've got to be here for every game possible.'

When **Rodney Bewes** is not appearing in TV series—remember him as one of the 'Likely Lads', followed by 'Dear Mother, Love Albert' and, more recently 'Albert'?—or in films or writing scripts, he is more than likely to be thinking about Chelsea. 'I've been a fan since the golden goalscoring days of Bobby Tambling. I used to stand at the Shed end, and only moved to a seat after a fan threw half an orange in my face!'

Actress **Judy Geeson** is Chelsea's 'girl next door'. Her Fulham Road studio flat looks out, back view, onto the Shed, and she comes to see Chelsea as often as possible between business engagements. She feels for her fellow-supporters, too—as she showed when serving late-night coffee to some who queued all night in protest at the transfer-listing of Peter Osgood last season.

Bill Gaunt, whose TV series have included 'The Challengers', 'Sergeant Cork' and 'The Champions', comes from Leeds, but has followed Chelsea regularly at home and often away since 1961, when his work first brought him to London and he lived off Fulham Road. These days his home is a little farther away, in Pimlico, but Bill has no Saturday afternoon parking problems when he gets to Stamford Bridge—he travels here by 'Chopper' bike!

John Mills is a Chelsea season-ticket holder; French singing star **Mireille Mathieu** likes to watch Chelsea when she is in London; **Honor Blackman,** though more of a Fulham follower, has often attended Stamford Bridge with her husband **Maurice Kaufmann**. Add such names as **Tom Courtenay**, **Harry Fowler**, **Kenny Lynch**, **Marty Feldman**, **Ben Warriss** and **John Slater**, and you have an absolute galaxy of stars from the world of Entertainment visiting Stamford Bridge on match days. Some come regularly, others occasionally; collectively, they make Chelsea the team with soccer's biggest show-business following. . . the club with star quality on the field and off.

21–Nil

To win the European Cup-Winners' Cup in Athens in May 1971, Chelsea defeated one of the most famous clubs in the world, Real Madrid. To begin their all-too-brief defence of it four months later, they faced a village team of amateurs who trained two nights a week in the hills of Luxembourg—by name Jeunesse Hautcharage. The eleven who lined up against Chelsea in the first leg on September 15 comprised five steel-workers, a stationmaster, student, hairdresser, technician, butcher and blacksmith, and some of them travelled to the game direct from work, by cycle!

The previous season Hautcharage had become the first Third Division club to win the Luxembourg Cup, beating hot favourites Jeunesse Esch 4–1 in the Final after extra time. For good measure, they also won promotion to the Second Division, but being drawn to play Chelsea, holders of the Cup-Winners' Cup, took them into a different world of football. The agricultural village of Hautcharage contributes no more than 704 inhabitants to Luxembourg's population of 334,000, and an average of barely three hundred normally watches them play on their rutted, roped-off pitch. Now, with so much interest in the visit of Chelsea, the match was switched to the National Stadium and, come the night, the attendance of 13,000 to see this soccer version of David versus Goliath was a record for the Grand Duchy of Luxembourg.

Before a ball was kicked, Jeunesse officials declared: 'We have no hope . . . if we lose 7–1, we'll be happy.' Chelsea welcomed the chance to rediscover their teamwork, which had gone sadly and astonishingly awry during the season's opening month, when eight League games produced no better reward than two wins, two draws and sixteenth place in the table.

But for Jeunesse, in their land of fairy-tale castles, this was to be no fairy-tale football adventure. True to expectations, it wasn't a match but the massacre of a side which included a midfield player who wore glasses; 20-year-old forward Guy Thill, a student born with only one arm; and with the four Welscher brothers to add a family touch to the line-up.

Six up at half-time, Chelsea soft-pedalled through the rest of the game, actually playing one period of 32 minutes without scoring. Finally, they settled for eight, and this was how they came:

1–0 (2 min): Cooke to Hollins on right and a quick cross to the far post, where Osgood brought the ball down with his left and cracked a right-footer past Fusulier.

2–0 (9 min): Houseman through the middle, finishing with a 20-yard shot through a ruck of players.

3–0 (28 min): Osgood helped himself to an easy header from Baldwin's centre.

4–0 (29 min): Houseman with another header after Osgood headed on Hudson's free-kick.

5–0 (37 min): Hollins, 25-yard left-foot 'special'.

6–0 (42 min): Osgood completed his hat-trick with a header from Cooke's cross.

7–0 (74 min): Baldwin with a glancing header just under the bar.

8–0 (81 min): Webb's header from eight yards beat both 'keeper and full-back on the line.

In addition, Osgood (twice) and Baldwin hit the post. It was Chelsea's highest single-leg victory in Europe and the first time they had scored eight in competitive football away from Stamford Bridge. From the 13,000 crowd, there were cheers for Jeunesse if they so much as crossed the half-way line. At the end their village band, some seventy strong, marched proudly off with trombones going full blare . . . and Chelsea fans awaited with relish the prospect of seeing the goal avalanche continue at Stamford Bridge two weeks later.

Eight away had killed the tie in one sense, but interest grew out of curiosity as to how many more Chelsea would score in the second leg and the records they might smash in so doing. With an eye to boosting the gate, the players declared well in advance that they were going for a ten-goal target; Peter Osgood personally set himself to get six and Ron Harris pledged that even he would find a place among the night's scorers.

The novelty of starting a match eight goals ahead would surely have appealed to Chelsea's two costly new captures,

Chris Garland and Steve Kember. But, having been signed after the August 15 deadline, they were reluctant figures in the crowd—a combined quarter of a million pounds' investment obliged by regulations to watch their new club re-write pages of the European record books.

For this was the night it rained goals at Stamford Bridge as never before:

1–0 (4 min): Osgood the scorer (his 100th first-team goal for Chelsea) from Hudson's low free-kick.

2–0 (6 min): Osgood again after the goalkeeper dropped Cooke's chipped cross.

3–0 (12 min): Hudson with a first-time right-footer from Cooke's right-wing centre.

4–0 (13 min): Hollins penalty, after Harris was brought down on edge of area.

5–0 (22 min): Webb back-header from Hudson's right-wing corner.

6–0 (42 min): Harris ended the game's longest goalless spell (20 minutes) with a cross-shot that went in off a defender, and so Chelsea repeated the six-nil half-time score in Luxembourg.

During the interval Jeunesse goalkeeper Lucien Fusulier, a 27-year-old mechanic, had three stitches put in a cut received over the left eye in a collision with Osgood. He decided to carry on, saying 'It is such an honour to be playing in London,' but, bravely though he played, he was as helpless as the rest of his defence to halt the Chelsea goal-machine as it continued its runaway pursuit of records through the second half:

7–0 (61 min): Baldwin's 20-yard right-foot drive meant that for the first time in eight years Stamford Bridge fans had seen Chelsea score seven—since Portsmouth were beaten 7–0 on promotion night in May 1963.

8–0 (63 min): Osgood header from Houseman cross.

9–0 (68 min): Baldwin back-header at near-post from Houseman centre—Chelsea's first 'nine' since 1907–08.

10–0 (77 min): Houseman with a powerful left-foot cross-shot—first ten-goal total in Chelsea history.

11–0 (80 min): Osgood header when Hollins' centre beat 'keeper—the goal that brought Chelsea the new record European aggregate of 19.

12–0 (88 min): Osgood's fifth of the night, and eighth of the tie—a header from Hudson's corner.

13–0 (90 min): A hat-trick for Baldwin with the last kick of the match from Houseman's centre.

Chelsea's thirteen goals—they also hit the woodwork five times through Houseman (three) and Hudson (twice)—came from the massive total of 54 goal attempts, 29 of them in the first half, 25 in the second. This was the individual analysis of those efforts:
Osgood 15 (5 goals, 4 saved, 4 wide, 2 high);
Baldwin 11 (3 goals, 6 saved, 2 wide);
Hudson 7 (1 goal, 1 hit bar, 1 hit post, 3 saved, 1 high);
Harris 6 (1 goal, 3 wide, 2 saved);
Hollins 6 (1 penalty goal, 1 hit 'keeper, 1 saved, 1 wide, 2 high);
Houseman 6 (1 goal, 2 hit post, 1 hit bar, 2 wide);
Webb 1 (1 goal); Boyle 1 (saved); Cooke 1 (blocked).

A crowd bonus of five pounds for every thousand spectators brought each Chelsea player a £135 pay-night from the attendance of 27,621. Peter Bonetti, the least occupied among them, collected an extra £5 from the wager Peter Osgood had made with him that he would personally score six!

Over the two matches, Hautcharage's lack of skill, pace and technique had been cruelly exposed, but they went down with courage and dignity, and at the finish the Chelsea team stood back and joined in the crowd's applause for the village amateurs from Luxembourg.

In the 16-year history of European competition, no club had ever been beaten 21–0 on aggregate, but Jeunesse were far from disconsolate when they flew home next day. Romain Schoder, their 31-year-old player-coach, stopper, sweeper and emergency goalkeeper, was still smiling as he said: 'A few months ago we never dreamed of playing the holders of the Cup-Winners' Cup, of coming to London to meet the famous Chelsea. For us it has been like a World Cup Final.' Their secretary, Rudi Weydert, added: 'It has been an honour and our great good luck to play Chelsea. We thank them for their fair play, and although we lost so heavily our players gained a lot of experience.'

When Chelsea were drawn against Jeunesse Hautcharage, officials, players and supporters alike asked 'Who are they?' They were asking a similar question when, two days after the 21–0 record-breaker, the second round paired them with Swedish part-timers Atvidaberg. But that was to be such a contrasting story . . . a shock ending to the club's participation in European competition for, at best, nearly two years.

Chelsea 21, Jeunesse Hautcharage 0
(8–0 away, 13–0 at home)

HOW THE RECORDS WENT

*The 21–0 aggregate was a new record for European football. Previous highest: 18–1 by Sporting Lisbon (2–0 away, 16–1 home) v. Apoel, Nicosia (Cup-Winners' Cup, 1963–64); 18–0 by Benfica (10–0 home, 8–0 away) v. Dudelange, Luxembourg (European Cup, 1965–66).
* Chelsea's aggregate beat the previous British record in Europe—16–0 (twice) by Leeds United: (9–0 away, 7–0 home v. Spora, Luxembourg in Fairs Cup, 1967–68; and 10–0 home, 6–0 away v. Lyn Oslo in European Cup, 1969–70).
* 13–0 in the second leg was Chelsea's biggest score in any competitive match. Previous highest: 9–2 v. Glossop (home) in Second Division, 1906–07; 9–1 v. Worksop (home) in F.A. Cup first round, 1907–08. 8–0 in the first leg against Jeunesse was Chelsea's record away score.
* Thirteen goals set a new single-leg British record in European football. Previous highest was ten by: Manchester United (10–0 v. Anderlecht, European Cup, 1956–57); Ipswich (10–0 v. Floriana, Malta, European Cup, 1962–63); Aberdeen (10–0 v. Reykjavik, Iceland, Cup Winners' Cup, 1967–68); Dunfermline (10–1 v. Apoel Nicosia, Cup-Winners' Cup, 1968–69); Leeds (10–0 v. Lyn Oslo, European Cup, 1969–70); Liverpool (10–0 v. Dundalk, Fairs Cup, 1969–70).
* Chelsea became the third club to total 13 in a first-class match in this country since the war. The others were Newcastle United (13–0 v. Newport County in Football League, Division 2, October 1946) and Tottenham Hotspur (13–2 v. Crewe Alexandra in F.A. Cup, February 1960).
* Peter Osgood's eight goals in the two legs against Jeunesse equalled the individual record for a European tie. Jose Altafini previously held it outright, for AC Milan against U.S. Luxembourg in the European Cup, (season 1962–63). Like Osgood he scored five at home, three away.
* Osgood's eight beat the previous British record in European football—seven by Ray Crawford (5 and 2) for Ipswich v. Floriana, Malta, in European Cup, 1962–63, and by Denis Law (4 and 3) for Manchester United v. Waterford, in European Cup, 1968–69.

PLAYER'S
PLANT HIRE
DUCKHAM

* Near misses: Osgood's five-goal performance in the second leg was one short of the European individual single-match total by Lothar Emmerich for Borussia Dortmund v. Floriana, Malta, in the Cup-Winners' Cup, 1965–66. Chelsea's 13 was three short of the record single-match total in European football (16–1 by Sporting Lisbon v. Apoel, Nicosia), in the Cup-Winners' Cup, 1963–64.

CHELSEA v. JEUNESSE HAUTCHARAGE

HOW THEY LINED UP

European Cup-Winners' Cup, 1971–72—1st. Round, 1st. Leg: Wednesday, 15th. September.
Jeunesse 0, Chelsea 8. Half-time: 0–6.
Jeunesse: Fusulier; Poos, Welscher (E), Schoder, Felten (Welscher, R), Welscher (J. P.) (Bottello), Frantzen, Welscher (L), Schrobiltgen, Thill (G), Kaiser.
Chelsea: Bonetti; Boyle, Harris, Hollins, Dempsey (Hinton), Webb, Cooke, Baldwin, Osgood, Hudson, Houseman.
Scorers: Osgood 3, Houseman 2, Hollins, Baldwin, Webb.
Referee: Mr. H. Biwersi (West Germany). Attendance: 13,000

2nd. Leg—Wednesday, 29th. September.
Chelsea 13, Jeunesse 0. Half-time: 6–0.
Chelsea: Bonetti; Boyle, Harris, Hollins, Webb, Hinton, Cooke, Baldwin, Osgood, Hudson, Houseman.
Scorers: Osgood 5, Baldwin 3, Hudson, Hollins (penalty), Webb, Harris, Houseman.
Jeunesse: Fusulier; Welscher (L), Frantzen, Welscher (E), Schoder (Simon), Battello, Welscher (R) (Thill, J. M.), Welscher (J. P.), Schrobiltgen, Thill (G), Kaiser.
Referee: Mr. R. Navarra (Malta). Attendance: 27,621.
Receipts: £10,449.

First of the eight in Luxembourg—scorer Peter Osgood.

A header by Peter Houseman brings the fourth of Chelsea's eight in the first leg abroad.

Osgood starts the festival of goals in the second leg at Stamford Bridge. It's his 100th in first-team football for Chelsea.

Tommy Baldwin launches the second half against Jeunesse at Stamford Bridge with a 20-yarder, the start of a personal hat-trick.

Records Section

League Appearances and Goalscorers for every Season in Chelsea's History (1905–72)

Season 1905–6 (Div. II—3rd)

P38, W22, D9, L7, Goals 90–37, Pts 53.

Appearances (24 Players)

Byrne, M.	3	McRoberts, R.	34
Copeland, D.	20	Miller, T.	24
Donaghy, C.	1	Moran, M.	34
Fletcher, J.	1	O'Hara, F.	1
Foulke, W.	34	Pearson, F.	29
Harris, C.	1	Porter, W.	1
Henderson, G.	3	Proudfoot, P.	4
Key, G.	33	Robertson, Jas.	16
Kirwan, J.	36	Robertson, J. T.	33
Mackie, R.	35	Walton, J.	13
McDermott, T.	22	Whiting, R.	1
McEwan, R.	19	Windridge, J. E.	20

Goalscorers: Pearson 18, Windridge 16, Robertson, Jas. 13, Kirwan 9, McRoberts 9, McDermott 7, Copeland 5, Moran 5, Robertson, J. T. 4, Donaghy 1, Key 1, Mackie 1, Opponent 1. **Total** 90.

Season 1906–7 (Div. II—2nd)

P38, W26, D5, L7, Goals 80–34, Pts 57.

Appearances (25 Players)

Birnie, E.	24	McCartney, D.	1
Brebner, R.	1	McDermott, T.	9
Bridgeman, W.	23	McRoberts, R.	35
Bush, R.	4	Miller, T.	38
Byrne, M.	1	Moran, M.	19
Copeland, D.	6	Porter, W.	1
Donaghy, C.	1	Proudfoot, P.	7
Frost, J. L.	19	Robertson, Jas.	13
Henderson, G.	37	Robertson, J. T.	3
Hildson, G.	32	Walton, J.	35
Key, G.	4	Whiting, R.	36
Kirwan, J.	35	Windridge, J. E.	31
Mackie, R.	3		

Goalscorers: Hilsdon 27, Windridge 16, Kirwan 8, Robertson, Jas. 8, Bridgeman 4, Copeland 4, Frost 4, McDermott 3, Moran 2, Birnie 1, Bush 1, Key 1, McRoberts 1. **Total** 80.

Season 1907–8 (Div. I—13th)

P38, W14, D8, L16, Goals 53–62, Pts 36.

Appearances (25 Players)

Birnie, E.	36	Mackie, R.	6
Brawn, W.	26	McRoberts, R.	20
Bridgeman, W.	18	Miller, T.	30
Cameron, J.	32	Moran, M.	10
Fairgray, N.	28	Proudfoot, P.	1
Frost, J.	3	Rouse, F.	20
Harding, A.	1	Stark, J.	30
Henderson, G.	14	Walton, J.	1
Hilsdon, G.	33	Whitehouse, B.	10
Humphreys, P.	11	Whiting, R.	15
Key, G.	13	Whitley, J.	23
Kirwan, J.	2	Windridge, J. E.	29
Lyon, F.	6		

Goalscorers: Hilsdon 24, Windridge 9, Rouse 6, Brawn 4, Stark 2, Birnie 1, Bridgeman 1, Fairgray 1, Henderson 1, Humphreys 1, Whitehouse 1, Opponents 2. **Total** 53.

Season 1908–9 (Div. I—11th)

P38, W14, D9, L15, Goals 56–61, Pts 37.

Appearances (25 Players)

Birnie, E.	31	Kennedy, G.	10
Brawn, W.	32	Key, G.	4
Bridgeman, W.	16	Mair, T.	4
Cameron, J.	35	McRoberts, R.	15
Cartwright, W.	12	Miller, T.	20
Douglas, A.	7	Reilly, E.	1
Downing, S.	6	Robinson, A.	2
Fairgray, N.	18	Rouse, F.	18
Freeman, C.	4	Walton, J.	12
Henderson, G.	6	Warren, B.	34
Hilsdon, G.	34	Whitley, J.	36
Holden, A.	4	Windridge, J. E.	34
Humphreys, P.	23		

Goalscorers: Hilsdon 25, Humphreys 9, Windridge 6, Rouse 5, Brawn 3, Bridgeman 3, Warren 3, Birnie 1, Douglas 1. **Total** 56.

Season 1909–10 (Div. I—19th)

P38, W11, D7, L20, Goals 47–70, Pts 29.

Appearances (34 Players)

Bettridge, W.	18	Jones, E.	18
Birnie, E.	10	Mair, T.	5
Bradshaw, J.	6	McConnell, E.	3
Brawn, W.	23	McEwan, M.	5
Bridgeman, W.	2	Ormiston, A.	24
Cameron, J.	26	Robinson, A.	1
Cartwright, W.	24	Saunders, J.	2
Dolby, H.	1	Smith, P.	1
Douglas, A.	14	Taylor, F.	20
Downing, S.	37	Walton, J.	5
Fairgray, N.	6	Warren, B.	17
Freeman, C.	9	Whitley, J.	35
Harding, A.	3	Whittingham, R.	3
Hilsdon, G.	15	Wileman, A.	14
Holden, A.	16	Williams, E.	6
Horn, G.	2	Windridge, J. E.	23
Humphreys, P.	11	Woodward, V. J.	13

Goalscorers: Windridge 6, Downing 5, Wileman 5, Woodward 5, Bradshaw 3, Brawn 3, Hilsdon 3, Humphreys 3, Jones 3, Douglas 2, Fairgray 2, Freeman 2, Holden 1, Mair 1, McEwan 1, Taylor 1, Whittingham 1. **Total** 47.

Season 1910–11 (Div. II—3rd)

P38, W20, D9, L9, Goals 71–35, Pts 49.

Appearances (24 Players)

Bettridge, W.	37	Jones, E.	3
Brawn, W.	12	McConnell, E.	18
Bridgeman, W.	15	McEwan, M.	28
Calderhead, D.	10	McKenzie, K.	1
Cameron, J.	34	Molyneux, J.	37
Cartwright, W.	5	Ormiston, A.	6
Dolby, H. R.	1	Taylor, F.	14
Douglas, A.	24	Warren, B.	31
Downing, S.	34	Whitley, J.	1
Fairgray, N.	2	Whittingham, R.	38
Freeman, C.	18	Windridge, J. E.	4
Hilsdon, G.	26	Woodward, V. J.	19

Goalscorers: Whittingham 30, Hilsdon 18, Douglas 6, Woodward 6, Bridgeman 2, Downing 2, Freeman 2, McEwan 2, Jones 1, Warren 1, Windridge 1. **Total** 71.

Season 1911–12 (Div. II—2nd)

P38, W24, D6, L8, Goals 64–34, Pts 54.

Appearances (26 Players)

Bettridge, W.	26	Hewitt, T.	8
Bridgeman, W.	26	Hilsdon, G.	10
Brown, W. Y.	3	Johnson, G.	2
Buchanan, R.	3	Molyneux, J.	12
Calderhead, D.	1	Ormiston, A.	37
Cameron, J.	36	Read, W.	3
Cartwright, W.	1	Taylor, F.	27
Dodd, G.	18	Thomson, R.	21
Douglas, A.	35	Warren, B.	10
Downing, S.	28	Whitley, J.	26
Fairgray, N.	10	Whittingham, R.	32
Freeman, C.	15	Windridge, J. E.	2
Harrow, J. H.	12	Woodward, V. J.	14

Goalscorers: Whittingham 26, Dodd 8, Freeman 7, Thomson 7, Bridgeman 6, Douglas 2, Taylor 2, Woodward 2, Brown 1, Downing 1, Hilsdon 1, Ormiston 1. **Total** 64.

Season 1912–13 (Div. I—18th)

P38, W11, D6, L21, Goals 51–73, Pts 28.

Appearances (28 Players)

Bettridge, W.	33	Harrow, J.	6
Brebner, R.	17	Harwood, J.	4
Bridgeman, W.	17	Hunter, G.	11
Brown, J.	11	Johnson, G.	2
Brown, W. Y.	6	Molyneux, J.	18
Calderhead, D.	16	Ormiston, A.	20
Cameron, J.	16	Sharp, J.	23
Cartwright, W.	2	Steer, W.	4
Dodd, G.	11	Taylor, F.	32
Douglas, A.	16	Thomson, R.	10
Downing, S.	25	Turnbull, J.	19
Fairgray, N.	9	Whitley, J.	3
Ford, H.	29	Whittingham, R.	20
Freeman, C.	11	Woodward, V. J.	27

Goalscorers: Woodward 10, Ford 9, Turnbull 8, Whittingham 7, Brown, J. 3, Freeman 3, Bridgeman 2, Fairgray 2, Brown, W. Y. 1, Downing 1, Hunter 1, Steer 1, Thomson 1, Opponents 2. **Total** 51.

Season 1913–14 (Div. I—8th)

P38, W16, D7, L15, Goals 46–55, Pts 39.

Appearances (29 Players)

Bettridge, W.	16	Marshall, O.	18
Bridgeman, W.	29	McFarlane, A.	3
Brittan, H.	2	Middelboe, N.	6
Brown, J.	3	Molyneux, J.	34
Calderhead, D.	7	Ormiston, A.	8
Downing, S.	4	Sharp, J.	21
Fairgray, N.	6	Taylor, F.	31
Ford, H.	37	Thomson, R.	9
Freeman, C.	21	Turnbull, J.	1
Halse, H. J.	30	Walker, A.	3
Harrow, J.	20	Whitley, J.	3
Hunter, G.	19	Whittingham, R.	20
Hampton, C.	1	Woodward, V. J.	27
Lake, G.	1	Woosnam, M.	3
Logan, T.	35		

Goalscorers: Halse 10, Ford 9, Whittingham 6, Freeman 5, Woodward 4, Bridgeman 2, Brittan 2, Logan 2, Walker 2, Calderhead 1, Hunter 1, Taylor 1, Thomson 1. **Total** 46.

Season 1914–15 (Div. I—19th)

P38, W8, D13, L17, Goals 51–65, Pts 29.

Appearances (23 Players)

Abrams, L.	31	Marshall, O.	11
Bettridge, W.	25	McFarlane, A.	1
Bridgeman, W.	1	McNeil, R.	37
Brittan, H.	9	Middelboe, N.	7
Brown, J.	2	Molyneux, J.	37
Croal, J.	27	Sharp, J.	17
Ford, H.	33	Taylor, F.	31
Freeman, C.	15	Thomson, R.	30
Halse, H. J.	27	Tye, E.	1
Hampton, C.	1	Walker, A.	12
Harrow, J.	22	Woodward, V. J.	6
Logan, T.	35		

Goalscorers: Thomson 12, Halse 10, Croal 6, Abrams 5, Logan 4, Ford 3, McNeil 3, Woodward 3, Brittan 2, Freeman 2, Brown 1. **Total** 51.

Season 1919–20 (Div. I—3rd)

P42, W22, D5, L15, Goals 56–51, Pts 49.

Appearances (26 Players)

Abrams, L.	13	Hampton, C.	15
Baxter, T.	1	Harrow, J.	39
Bettridge, W.	41	Lee, J.	4
Brittan, H.	13	Logan, T.	22
Browning, J.	5	Marshall, O.	5
Cock, J.	25	McNeil, R.	26
Croal, J.	32	Middelboe, N.	9
Dale, G.	36	Molyneux, J.	27
Dickie, W.	28	Sharp, B.	11
Ford, H.	30	Spottiswood, R.	1
Freeman, C.	2	Walker, A.	3
Gallon, J.	2	Whittingham, R.	6
Halse, H. J.	31	Wilding, H.	35

Goalscorers: Cock 21, Croal 6, Wilding 4, Brittan 3, Ford 3, Halse 3, McNeil 3, Sharp 3, Abrams 2, Harrow 2, Browning 1, Dale 1, Lee 1, Logan 1, Whittingham 1, Opponent 1. **Total** 56.

Season 1920–21 (Div. I—18th)

P42, W13, D13, L16, Goals 48–58, Pts 39.

Appearances (29 Players)

Ashford, J.	4	Langton, J.	1
Barrett, F.	10	Lee, J.	2
Bell, J. B.	6	Linfoot, F.	13
Bettridge, W.	28	Logan, T.	15
Cameron, D.	13	McKenzie, K.	3
Cock, J.	32	McNeil, R.	39
Croal, J.	33	Meehan, T.	19
Dale, G.	8	Middelboe, N.	14
Dickie, W.	7	Molyneux, J.	36
Ferguson, E.	1	Priestley, J.	1
Ferris, J.	27	Sharp, B.	8
Ford, H.	23	Thomson, R.	13
Halse, H. J.	8	Ward, J.	12
Hampton, C.	6	Wilding, H.	40
Harrow, J.	40		

Goalscorers: Cock 12, Ferris 8, Croal 7, McNeil 6, Ford 4, Wilding 3, Bell 2, Cameron 2, Harrow 2, Thomson 2. **Total** 48.

Season 1921–22 (Div. I—9th)

P42, W17, D12, L13, Goals 40–43, Pts 46.

Appearances (28 Players)

Ashford, J.	2	Hoddinott, F.	23
Baker, B. H.	23	Langton, J.	2
Barrett, F.	9	Linfoot, F.	2
Bell, J.	24	Marsh, W.	1
Cameron, D.	13	McKenzie, K.	18
Cock, J.	31	McNeil, R.	42
Croal, J.	21	Meehan, T.	37
Dale, G.	5	Middelboe, N.	5
Ferris, J.	6	Molyneux, J.	9
Finlayson, W.	1	Sharp, B.	21
Ford, H.	29	Smith, G. W.	35
Hampton, C.	9	Smith, S.	20
Harrow, J.	38	Ward, J.	2
Haywood, J.	5	Wilding, H.	29

Goalscorers: Cock 13, Sharp 7, Bell 5, Croal 3, Ford 3, Hoddinott 3, McNeil 2, Baker 1, Harrow 1, Haywood 1, Smith, S. 1. **Total** 40.

Season 1922–23 (Div. I—19th)

P42, W9, D18, L15, Goals 45–53, Pts 36.

Appearances (25 Players)

Armstrong, J.	14	Hoddinott, F.	8
Ashford, J.	1	Lee, J.	1
Baker, B. H.	17	Linfoot, F.	14
Bell, J.	12	McNeil, R.	41
Bennett, W.	1	Meehan, T.	42
Cameron, D.	25	Priestley, J.	20
Cock, J.	11	Sharp, B.	25
Ferguson, E.	10	Smith, G. W.	42
Ford, H.	37	Smith, S.	2
Frew, J.	14	Thain, A.	9
Hampton, C.	25	Whitton, W.	6
Harrow, J.	40	Wilding, H.	29
Haywood, J.	16		

Goalscorers: Ford 10, Sharp 10, Armstrong 7, McNeil 4, Meehan 3, Wilding 3, Bell 2, Whitton 2, Cock 1, Haywood 1, Hoddinott 1, Priestley 1. **Total** 45.

Season 1923–24 (Div. I—21st)

P42, W9, D14, L19, Goals 31–53, Pts 32.

Appearances (28 Players)

Armstrong, J.	13	Hampton, C.	22
Baker, B. H.	11	Harrow, J.	38
Barrett, F.	4	Haywood, J.	2
Bennett, W.	4	Linfoot, F.	5
Bower, A. G.	3	Marsh, W.	9
Brown, W.	11	McNeil, R.	29
Cameron, D.	11	Meehan, T.	26
Castle, S.	24	Miller, H.	32
Crawford, J.	21	Priestley, J.	40
Duffy, B.	1	Smith, G. W.	39
Ferguson, W.	27	Thain, A.	6
Finlayson, W.	4	Whitton, W.	10
Ford, H.	4	Wilding, H.	39
Frew, J.	8	Wilson, A.	19

Goalscorers: Wilson 5, Brown 4, Wilding 4, Crawford 3, Miller 3, Armstrong 2, Castle 2, Priestley 2, Ferguson 1, Finlayson 1, Linfoot 1, Meehan 1, Thain 1, Whitton 1. **Total** 31.

Season 1924–25 (Div. II—5th)

P42, W16, D15, L11, Goals 51–37, Pts 47.

Appearances (28 Players)

Armstrong, J.	1	McNeil, R.	35
Ashford, J.	1	Miller, H.	30
Baker, B. H.	28	Morrison, W.	1
Barrett, F.	7	Odell, L.	2
Brown, W.	18	Plum, S.	17
Cameron, D.	11	Priestley, J.	35
Castle, S.	8	Rodger, G.	10
Crawford, J.	26	Sales, A.	5
Duffy, B.	1	Smith, G. W.	40
Ferguson, W.	30	Thain, A.	2
Frew, J.	18	Turnbull, R.	9
Harrow, J.	34	Whitton, W.	22
Jenkins, R.	4	Wilding, H.	17
McKenna, P.	14	Wilson, A.	36

Goalscorers: Whitton 16, Wilson 10, Brown 7, Miller 6, McNeil 3, Turnbull 3, Ferguson 2, Crawford 1, Plum 1, Priestley 1, Wilding 1. **Total** 51.

Season 1925–26 (Div. II—3rd)

P42, W19, D14, L9, Goals 76–49, Pts 52.

Appearances (24 Players)

Armstrong, J.	1	Miller, H.	20
Baker, B. H.	13	Odell, L.	1
Barrett, F.	28	Pearson, G.	1
Bower, A. G.	6	Plum, S.	9
Brown, W.	12	Priestley, J.	39
Crawford, J.	36	Rodger, G.	32
Duffy, B.	1	Smith, G. W.	34
Ferguson, W.	27	Stone, G.	22
Frew, J.	2	Thain, A.	32
Harrow, J.	15	Turnbull, R.	36
McKenna, P.	29	Wilding, H.	19
McNeil, R.	24	Wilson, A.	23

Goalscorers: Turnbull 29, Thain 15, Wilson 7, Barrett 5, McNeil 5, Priestley 4, Crawford 3, Miller 2, Stone 2, Wilding 2, Brown 1, Opponent 1. **Total** 76.

Season 1926–27 (Div. II—4th)

P42, W20, D12, L10, Goals 62–52, Pts 52.

Appearances (20 Players)

Barrett, F.	6	Priestley, J.	39
Brown, W.	11	Rodger, G.	20
Crawford, J.	39	Sales, A.	1
Ferguson, W.	42	Smith, G. W.	42
Law, T.	36	Stone, G.	3
Miller, H.	20	Thain, A.	39
Millington, S.	32	Townrow, J.	9
McKenna, P.	10	Turnbull, R.	32
McNeil, R.	6	Wilding, H.	16
Pearson, G.	35	Wilson, A.	24

Goalscorers: Turnbull 17, Thain 14, Brown 7, Priestley 6, Crawford 3, Ferguson 3, Miller 3, Pearson 3, Wilson 3, Barrett 1, McNeil 1, Wilding 1. **Total** 62.

Season 1927–28 (Div. II—3rd)

P42, W23, D8, L11, Goals 75–45, Pts 54.

Appearances (26 Players)

Anderson, G.	5	Pearson, G.	35
Biswell, G.	5	Priestley, J.	17
Brown, W.	2	Rodger, G.	13
Crawford, J.	39	Russell, W.	2
Ferguson, C.	1	Sales, A.	1
Ferguson, W.	41	Smith, G. W.	40
Irving, S.	11	Thain, A.	31
Jackson, W.	8	Thompson, J.	29
Law, T.	38	Townrow, J.	25
McKenna, P.	2	Turnbull, R.	3
Miller, H.	11	Wilding, H.	17
Millington, S.	40	Williams, W.	2
Odell, L.	6	Wilson, A.	38

Goalscorers: Thompson 25, Wilson 11, Thain 10, Crawford 6, Pearson 4, Priestley 4, Wilding 4, Jackson 2, Turnbull 2, Biswell 1, Brown 1, Ferguson, W. 1, Irving 1, Law 1, Miller 1, Rodger 1. **Total** 75.

Season 1928–29 (Div. II—9th)

P42, W17, D10, L15, Goals 64–65, Pts 44.

Appearances (24 players)

Anderson, G.	4	Miller, H.	22
Bishop, S.	21	Millington, S.	38
Biswell, G.	18	Odell, L.	7
Carr, J.	1	Pearson, G.	32
Crawford, J.	27	Rodger, G.	2
Elliott, S.	14	Russell, W.	13
Ferguson, W.	22	Smith, G. W.	37
Irving, S.	32	Thain, A.	23
Jackson, W.	9	Thompson, J.	8
Law, T.	39	Townrow, J.	41
McKenna, P.	4	Weaver, R.	11
Meredith, J.	16	Wilson, A.	21

Goalscorers: Biswell 9, Wilson 9, Thompson 8, Pearson 6, Meredith 5, Miller 4, Thain 4, Weaver 4, Elliott 3, Bishop 2, Crawford 2, Jackson 2, Odell 2, Townrow 2, Irving 1, Law 1. **Total** 64.

Season 1929–30 (Div. II—2nd)

P42, W22, D11, L9, Goals 74–46, Pts 55.

Appearances (23 Players)

Bishop, S.	36	Mills, G.	20
Biswell, G.	1	Millington, S.	38
Crawford, J.	32	Odell, L.	13
Elliott, S.	16	Pearson, G.	38
Ferguson, W.	11	Rodger, G.	28
Higgs, F.	2	Russell, W.	20
Irving, S.	17	Smith, G. W.	30
Jackson, W.	7	Thain, A.	2
Law, T.	41	Townrow, J.	14
McKenna, P.	2	Weaver, R.	8
Meredith, J.	7	Wilson, A.	39
Miller, H.	40		

Goalscorers: Mills 14, Miller 13, Pearson 12, Wilson 10, Elliott 6, Crawford 4, Weaver 4, Bishop 3, Ferguson 2, Jackson 2, Irving 1, Meredith 1, Rodger 1, Opponent 1. **Total** 74.

Season 1930–31 (Div. I—12th)

P42, W15, D10, L17, Goals 64–67, Pts 40.

Appearances (25 Players)

Barber, G.	11	McKenna, P.	1
Bishop, S.	22	Miller, H.	10
Carter, R.	1	Millington, S.	40
Cheyne, A.	34	Mills, G.	7
Crawford, J.	32	Odell, L.	23
Donald, A.	12	Pearson, G.	26
Ferguson, W.	25	Rankin, J.	6
Gallacher, H.	30	Rodger, G.	14
Irving, S.	20	Russell, W.	17
Jackson, A.	29	Smith, G. W.	11
Jackson, W.	2	Townrow, J.	27
Law, T.	27	Wilson, A.	34
Macintosh, S.	1		

Goalscorers: Gallacher 14, Jackson, A. 10, Cheyne 9, Law 6, Odell 5, Crawford 4, Pearson 4, Wilson 4, Irving 2, Donald 1, Miller 1, Mills 1, Rankin 1, Russell 1, Townrow 1. **Total** 64.

Season 1931–32 (Div. I—12th)

P42, W16, D8, L18, Goals 69–73, Pts 40.

Appearances (26 Players)

Barber, G.	33	Miller, H.	22
Bishop, S.	17	Millington, S.	35
Carter, R.	16	Mills, G.	14
Cheyne, A.	19	Odell, L.	11
Chitty, W.	6	O'Dowd, P.	24
Crawford, J.	21	Pearson, G.	27
Donald, A.	12	Rankin, J.	24
Ferguson, W.	21	Russell, W.	24
Gallacher, H.	36	Smith, G. W.	1
Hope, J.	1	Townrow, J.	14
Irving, S.	9	Weaver, R.	1
Jackson, A.	36	Wilson, A.	4
Law, T.	27	Woodley, V.	7

Goalscorers: Gallacher 24, Jackson 15, Mills 8, Pearson 4, Rankin 4, Miller 3, Russell 3, Ferguson 2, Carter 1, Cheyne 1, Chitty 1, Law 1, Opponents 2. **Total** 69.

Season 1932–33 (Div. I—18th)

P42, W14, D7, L21, Goals 63–73, Pts 35.

Appearances (25 Players)

Allum, L.	13	Law, T.	33
Barber, G.	24	Macaulay, R.	10
Bishop, S.	7	Miller, H.	17
Carter, R.	1	Mills, G.	31
Chitty, W.	6	Oakton, A.	34
Craig, A.	19	Odell, L.	17
Crawford, J.	15	O'Dowd, P.	36
Dudley, S.	1	Pearson, G.	3
Ferguson, W.	17	Prout, S.	16
Gallacher, H.	36	Rankin, J.	29
Gibson, G.	13	Russell, W.	31
Griffiths, R.	2	Woodley, V.	42
Horton, J.	9		

Goalscorers: Gallacher 19, Mills 13, Oakton 8, Gibson 5, Rankin 4, Miller 3, Prout 3, Chitty 2, Horton 2, Law 2, Russell 1, Opponent 1. **Total** 63.

Season 1933–34 (Div. I—19th)

P42, W14, D8, L20, Goals 67–69, Pts 36.

Appearances (26 Players)

Allum, L.	14	Law, T.	25
Argue, J.	1	Macaulay, R.	13
Barber, G.	31	Miller, H.	23
Chitty, W.	5	Mills, G.	24
Copeland, J.	1	Mitchell, W.	2
Craig, A.	30	Oakton, A.	41
Gallacher, H.	23	Odell, L.	14
Gibson, G.	32	O'Dowd, P.	20
Gregg, R.	28	O'Hare, J.	1
Griffiths, R.	1	Priestley, T.	23
Horton, J.	30	Rankin, J.	3
Hutcheson, J.	6	Russell, W.	29
Jackson, J.	6	Woodley, V.	36

Goalscorers: Mills 14, Gallacher 13, Oakton 12, Gibson 9, Horton 8, Law 4, Gregg 2, Chitty 1, Copeland 1, Miller 1, Priestley 1, Opponent 1. **Total** 67.

Season 1934–35 (Div. I—12th)

P42, W16, D9, L17, Goals 73–82, Pts 41.

Appearances (25 Players)

Allum, L.	22	Hutcheson, J.	11
Argue, J.	27	Jackson, J.	27
Bambrick, J.	21	Macaulay, R.	38
Barber, G.	39	Miller, H.	34
Barraclough, W.	29	Mills, G.	20
Burgess, H.	10	Mitchell, W.	4
Cheyne, A.	3	Odell, L.	5
Copeland, J.	1	O'Hare, J.	2
Craig, A.	42	Oakton, A.	8
Gallacher, H.	7	Russell, W.	14
Gibson, G.	23	Spence, R.	34
Gregg, R.	13	Woodley, V.	15
Horton, J.	13		

Goalscorers: Spence 19, Bambrick 15, Mills 8, Barraclough 6, Argue 5, Horton 4, Burgess 3, Gregg 3, Gallacher 2, Cheyne 1, Gibson 1, Hutcheson 1, Macaulay 1, Oakton 1, Russell 1, Opponents 2. **Total** 73.

Season 1935–36 (Div. I—8th)

P42, W15, D13, L14, Goals 65–72, Pts 43.

Appearances (26 Players)

Allum, L.	12	Hutcheson, J.	5
Argue, J.	9	Jackson, J.	10
Bambrick, J.	25	Law, T.	23
Barber, G.	27	Macaulay, R.	5
Barraclough, W.	30	Mayes, A.	2
Burgess, H.	31	Mills, G.	19
Cheyne, A.	6	Miller, H.	34
Chitty, W.	1	Mitchell, W.	31
Craig, A.	41	Oakton, A.	8
Gibson, G.	33	O'Hare, J.	27
Gregg, R.	3	Odell, L.	2
Griffiths, R.	1	Spence, R.	40
Horton, J.	5	Woodley, V.	32

Goalscorers: Bambrick 15, Spence 13, Burgess 11, Mills 11, Gibson 4, Oakton 3, Argue 2, Barraclough 2, Allum 1, Cheyne 1, Horton 1, Miller 1. **Total** 65.

Season 1936–37 (Div. I—13th)

P42, W14, D13, L15, Goals 52–55, Pts 41.

Appearances (24 Players)

Allum, L.	4	Griffiths, R.	1
Argue, J.	32	Horton, J.	2
Bambrick, J.	10	Jackson, J.	1
Barber, G.	41	Miller, H.	16
Barraclough, W.	15	Mills, G.	32
Buchanan, P.	1	Mitchell, W.	27
Burgess, H.	29	Oakton, A.	16
Chitty, W.	8	O'Hare, J.	36
Craig, A.	41	Smale, D.	6
Foss, S. R.	4	Spence, R.	39
Gibson, G.	19	Weaver, S.	38
Gregg, R.	3	Woodley, V.	41

Goalscorers: Mills 22, Spence 8, Argue 6, Burgess 4, Gibson 3, Oakton 3, Weaver 3, Bambrick 2, Chitty 1. **Total** 52.

Season 1937–38 (Div. I—10th)

P42, W14, D13, L15, Goals 65–65, Pts 41.

Appearances (28 Players)

Allum, L.	15	Jackson, J.	2
Argue, J.	21	Law, T.	4
Bambrick, J.	3	Mayes, A.	4
Barber, G.	29	Miller, H.	6
Barkas, E.	18	Mills, G.	27
Bidewell, S.	4	Mitchell, W.	21
Buchanan, P.	33	O'Hare, J.	22
Burgess, H.	36	Payne, J.	10
Chitty, W.	19	Sherbourne, J.	5
Craig, A.	7	Smale, D.	2
Foss, S. R.	11	Smith, A. J.	11
Gibson, G.	9	Spence, R.	28
Gregg, R.	1	Weaver, S.	39
Griffiths, R.	35	Woodley, V.	40

Goalscorers: Mills 13, Chitty 11, Argue 9, Burgess 7, Buchanan 6, Payne 4, Spence 4, Foss 3, Bidewell 2, Mitchell 2, Bambrick 1, Gibson 1, Weaver 1, Opponent 1. **Total** 65.

Season 1938–39 (Div. I—20th)

P42, W12, D9, L21, Goals 64–80, Pts 33.

Appearances (25 Players)

Alexander, D.	1	Mayes, A.	6
Allum, L.	13	Mills, G.	26
Argue, J.	27	Mitchell, W.	23
Barber, G.	27	O'Hare, J.	14
Barkas, E.	9	Payne, J.	26
Buchanan, P.	5	Reid, E.	1
Burgess, H.	36	Salmond, R.	24
Craig, A.	16	Smale, D.	1
Foss, S. R.	11	Smith, A. J.	34
Gibson, G.	1	Spence, R.	41
Griffiths, R.	2	Weaver, S.	39
Hanson, A.	37	Woodley, V.	39
Jackson, J.	3		

Goalscorers: Payne 17, Mills 12, Spence 11, Burgess 8, Hanson 8, Argue 7, Allum 1. **Total** 64.

Season 1946–47 (Div. I—15th)

P42, W16, D7, L19, Goals 69–84, Pts 39.

Appearances (28 Players)

Argue, J.	1	Machin, A.	37
Bain, J.	9	McInnes, J.	3
Bathgate, S.	7	Medhurst, H.	20
Davidson, A.	2	Paton, J.	18
Dickie, M.	1	Richardson, F.	2
Dolding, D. L.	17	Robertson, W. H.	22
Foss, S. R.	12	Russell, R.	2
Galloway, J.	3	Spence, R.	33
Goddard, R.	5	Steffen, W.	15
Goulden, L.	38	Tennant, A.	1
Harris, J.	41	Walker, T.	39
Lawton, T.	34	White, A.	13
Lewis, F.	7	Williams, R.	9
Macaulay, J.	30	Winter, D.	41

Goalscorers: Lawton 26, Goulden 10, Walker 9, Machin 7, Spence 7, Paton 3, Williams 2, Argue 1, Bain 1, Dolding 1, Macaulay 1, McInnes 1. **Total** 69.

Season 1947–48 (Div. I—18th)

P42, W14, D9, L19, Goals 53–71, Pts 37.

Appearances (29 Players)

Armstrong, K.	42	Jones, T. B.	11
Bathgate, S.	32	Lawton, T.	8
Bentley, R.	14	Lewis, F.	12
Billington, H.	12	Macaulay, J.	15
Bowie, J.	22	Machin, A.	16
Campbell, R.	32	McInnes, J.	15
Dickson, W.	1	McKnight, P.	1
Dolding, D. L.	9	Medhurst, H.	27
Dyke, C.	13	Robertson, W. H.	15
Foss, S. R.	3	Simner, J.	1
Galloway, J.	1	Spence, R.	6
Goddard, R.	9	Walker, T.	37
Goulden, L.	27	White, A.	4
Harris, J.	41	Winter, D.	28
Hughes, W.	8		

Goalscorers: Armstrong 11, Campbell 11, Walker 7, Bowie 5, Goulden 4, Lawton 4, Bentley 3, Billington 2, Harris 2, Dolding 1, Dyke 1, Goddard 1, Machin 1. **Total** 53.

Season 1948–49 (Div. I—13th)

P42, W12, D14, L16, Goals 69–68, Pts 38.

Appearances (25 Players)

Armstrong, K.	25	Lewis, F.	3
Bathgate, S.	17	Macaulay, J.	36
Bentley, R.	40	McInnes, J.	18
Billington, H.	16	McKnight, P.	2
Bowie, J.	22	Medhurst, H.	26
Campbell, R.	36	Mitchell, F.	11
Dickson, W.	2	Pickering, P.	16
Dyke, C.	2	Tennant, A.	1
Goulden, L.	20	Walker, T.	21
Gray, W.	2	Warren, R.	1
Harris, J.	41	Williams, R.	13
Hughes, W.	38	Winter, D.	25
Jones, T. B.	28		

Goalscorers: Bentley 20, Bowie 7, Campbell 7, Walker 7, Jones 6, Macaulay 4, McInnes 4, Billington 3, Williams 3, Armstrong 1, Goulden 1, Harris 1, Mitchell 1, Opponents 4. **Total** 69.

Season 1949–50 (Div. I—13th)

P42, W12, D16, L14, Goals 58–65, Pts 40.

Appearances (23 Players)

Armstrong, K.	41	Jones, T. B.	6
Bathgate, S.	10	Macaulay, J.	5
Bentley, R.	39	McInnes, J.	1
Billington, H.	35	McKnight, P.	1
Bowie, J.	16	Medhurst, H.	41
Campbell, R.	35	Mitchell, F.	33
Dickson, W.	3	Pickering, P.	1
Goulden, L.	14	Saunders, F. J.	3
Gray, W.	39	Willemse, S.	18
Harris, J.	39	Williams, R.	21
Hughes, W.	24	Winter, D.	32
Jenkins, T. F.	5		

Goalscorers: Bentley 17, Billington 17, Williams 5, Bowie 4, Campbell 4, Harris 3, Goulden 2, Gray 2, Jones 2, Opponents 2. **Total** 58.

Season 1950–51 (Div. I—20th)

P42, W12, D8, L22, Goals 53–65, Pts 32.

Appearances (25 Players)

Armstrong, K.	40	McKnight, P.	5
Bathgate, S.	34	Medhurst, H.	28
Bentley, R.	38	Mitchell, F.	27
Billington, H.	20	Parsons, E.	5
Bowie, J.	16	Pickering, P.	10
Campbell, R.	33	Robertson, W. G.	4
Dickson, W.	20	Saunders, F. J.	7
Dyke, C.	9	Smith, R.	16
Gray, W.	31	Tickridge, S.	8
Harris, J.	36	Willemse, S.	15
Hinshelwood, W.	12	Williams, R.	13
Hughes, W.	23	Winter, D.	5
Jones, T. B.	7		

Goalscorers: Bentley 8, Smith 7, Billington 6, Campbell 6, Gray 6, Harris 5, Armstrong 4, Williams 3, Bowie 2, Dickson 1, Dyke 1, Hinshelwood 1, Jones 1, Willemse 1, Opponent 1. **Total** 53.

Season 1951–52 (Div. I—19th)

P42, W14, D8, L20, Goals 52–72, Pts 36.

Appearances (26 Players)

Allister, J.	3	Medhurst, H.	1
Armstrong, K.	37	Mitchell, F.	4
Bathgate, S.	32	Oelofse, R.	3
Bentley, R.	32	Parsons, E.	11
Campbell, R.	32	Randall, E.	3
D'Arcy, S.	21	Robertson, W. G.	41
Dickson, W.	37	Saunders, F. J.	13
Gray, W.	42	Smith, J.	16
Harris, J.	26	Smith, R.	32
Hughes, H.	1	Tickridge, S.	41
Jones, T. B.	3	Tuck, P.	3
Leadbetter, J.	3	Willemse, S.	11
McKnight, P.	12	Williams, R.	2

Goalscorers: Bentley 12, D'Arcy 12, Smith, R. 11, Campbell 5, Smith, J. 3, Armstrong 2, Jones 2, Allister 1, Gray 1, Parsons 1, Randall 1, Tuck 1. **Total** 52.

Season 1952–53 (Div. I—19th)

P42, W12, D11, L19, Goals 56–66, Pts 35.

Appearances (28 Players)

Allister, J.	1	Lewis, J. L.	9
Armstrong, K.	41	McKnight, P.	4
Bathgate, S.	3	McNichol, J.	39
Bentley, R.	37	Oelofse, R.	5
Blunstone, F.	11	Parsons, E.	33
Campbell, R.	18	Robertson, W. G.	27
D'Arcy, S.	2	Saunders, F. J.	20
Dicks, A.	1	Smith, J.	1
Dickson, W.	38	Smith, R.	7
Edwards, R.	12	Spector, M.	2
Gray, W.	32	Stubbs, L.	5
Greenwood, R.	11	Thomson, C.	15
Harris, J.	36	Tickridge, S.	12
Lewis, F.	1	Willemse, S.	39

Goalscorers: Bentley 12, McNichol 11, Parsons 8, Lewis, J. L. 4, Campbell 3, Dickson 3, Gray 3, Harris 3, Blunstone 2, Edwards 2, Armstrong 1, McKnight 1, Smith, R. 1, Opponents 2. **Total** 56.

Season 1953–54 (Div. I—8th)

P42, W16, D12, L14, Goals 74–68, Pts 44.

Appearances (24 Players)

Armstrong, K.	40	McNichol, J.	41
Bentley, R.	41	Parsons, E.	29
Blunstone, F.	32	Robertson, W. G.	34
Bowman, A.	1	Saunders, D.	33
Campbell, R.	2	Saunders, F. J.	9
Collins, R. M.	1	Sillett, P.	12
Dicks, A.	2	Smith, J.	2
Greenwood, R.	33	Smith, R.	8
Harris, J.	32	Spector, M.	1
Kell, L.	3	Stubbs, L.	30
Lewis, J. L.	20	Thomson, C.	7
McKnight, P.	8	Willemse, S.	41

Goalscorers: Bentley 21, McNichol 18, Lewis 9, Parsons 9, Stubbs 9, Blunstone 3, Armstrong 2, Saunders, D. 1, Opponents 2. **Total** 74.

Season 1954–55 (Div. I—Champions)

P42, W20, D12, L10, Goals 81–57, Pts 52.

Appearances (20 Players)

Armstrong, K.	39	O'Connell, S.	10
Bentley, R.	41	Parsons, E.	42
Blunstone, F.	23	Robertson, W. G.	26
Brabrook, P.	3	Saunders, D.	42
Dicks, A.	1	Sillett, P.	21
Edwards, R.	1	Smith, R.	4
Greenwood, R.	21	Stubbs, L.	27
Harris, J.	31	Thomson, C.	16
Lewis, J. L.	17	Wicks, M. S.	21
McNichol, J.	40	Willemse, S.	36

Goalscorers: Bentley 21, McNichol 14, Parsons 11, O'Connell 7, Lewis 6, Sillett 6, Stubbs 5, Blunstone 3, Armstrong 1, Saunders 1, Wicks 1, Willemse 1, Opponents 4. **Total** 81.

Season 1955–56 (Div. I—16th)

P42, W14, D11, L17, Goals 64–77, Pts 39.

Appearances (26 Players)

Armstrong, K.	24	Nicholas, B.	10
Bellett, W.	2	O'Connell, S.	6
Bentley, R.	38	Parsons, E.	33
Blunstone, F.	41	Robertson, W. G.	34
Brabrook, P.	18	Saunders, D.	37
Casey, L.	7	Sillett, P.	41
Compton, J.	1	Smith, R.	7
Dicks, A.	4	Stubbs, L.	17
Harris, J.	3	Thomson, C.	8
Kitchener, R.	1	Tindall, R.	15
Lewis, J. L.	9	Whittaker, R.	1
McNichol, J.	24	Wicks, M. S.	42
Mortimore, J.	1	Willemse, S.	38

Goalscorers: Bentley 14, Stubbs 10, Parsons 7, Tindall 7, Blunstone 6, O'Connell 4, Smith 4, Brabrook 3, McNichol 2, Lewis 2, Sillett 2, Dicks 1, Opponents 2. **Total** 64.

Season 1956–57 (Div. I—13th)

P42, W13, D13, L16, Goals 73–73, Pts 39.

Appearances (29 Players)

Allen, L.	19	Matthews, R.	22
Armstrong, K.	33	McNichol, J.	24
Bellett, W.	10	Mortimore, J.	2
Bentley, R.	4	Nicholas, A.	20
Berry, P.	2	Nicholas, B.	7
Blunstone, F.	27	Parsons, E.	5
Brabrook, P.	38	Robertson, W. G.	20
Casey, L.	3	Saunders, D.	41
Dicks, A.	19	Sillett, J.	2
Gibbs, D.	4	Sillett, P.	30
Harrison, M.	1	Stubbs, L.	18
Laverick, R.	6	Tindall, R.	26
Livingstone, W.	12	Whittaker, R.	11
Lewis, J. L.	18	Wicks, M. S.	8
MacFarlane, I.	30		

Goalscorers: McNichol 10, Tindall 10, Lewis 9, Stubbs 7, Brabrook 6, Nicholas, A. 6, Saunders 6, Allen 5, Blunstone 5, Armstrong 2, Sillett, P. 2, Gibbs 1, Nicholas, B. 1, Parsons 1, Opponents 2. **Total** 73.

Season 1957–58 (Div. I—11th)

P42, W15, D12, L15, Goals 83–79, Pts 42.

Appearances (28 Players)

Allen, L.	9	Livingstone, W.	8
Bellett, W.	20	MacFarlane, I.	10
Berry, P.	1	Matthews, R.	42
Block, M.	20	McNichol, J.	13
Brabrook, P.	41	Mortimore, J.	39
Casey, L.	21	Nicholas, A.	11
Cliss, D.	9	Nicholas, B.	9
Compton, J.	3	Saunders, D.	31
Dicks, A.	6	Scott, M.	9
Gibbs, D.	4	Sillett, J.	1
Greaves, J.	35	Sillett, P.	40
Harrison, M.	1	Stubbs, L.	13
Laverick, R.	1	Tindall, R.	36
Lewis, J. L.	17	Whittaker, R.	12

Goalscorers: Greaves 22, Tindall 16, Brabrook 8, Lewis 8, Nicholas, A. 6, Block 4, McNichol 4, Sillett, P. 4, Allen 3, Stubbs 3, Bellett 1, Cliss 1, Gibbs 1, Mortimore 1, Opponent 1. **Total** 83.

Season 1958–59 (Div. I—14th)

P42, W18, D4, L20, Goals 77–98, Pts 40.

Appearances (28 Players)

Allen, L.	11	Huxford, C.	6
Anderton, S.	8	Matthews, R.	32
Bellett, W.	3	Mortimore, J.	37
Block, M.	13	Nicholas, A.	21
Blunstone, F.	21	Robertson, W. G.	10
Brabrook, P.	39	Saunders, D.	19
Bridges, B.	2	Scott, M.	34
Casey, L.	3	Shellito, K.	2
Cliss, D.	3	Sillett, J.	27
Crowther, S.	21	Sillett, P.	35
Gibbs, D.	8	Stubbs, L.	2
Greaves, J.	42	Tambling, R.	1
Harrison, M.	16	Tindall, R.	29
Holton, P.	1	Whittaker, R.	16

Goalscorers: Greaves 32, Tindall 13, Brabrook 7, Sillett, P. 7, Nicholas 5, Allen 3, Blunstone 2, Harrison 2, Block 1, Bridges 1, Gibbs 1, Mortimore 1, Saunders 1, Tambling 1. **Total** 77.

Season 1959–60 (Div. I—18th)

P42, W14, D9, L19, Goals 76–91, Pts 37.

Appearances (29 Players)

Allen, L.	5	Livesey, C.	25
Anderton, S.	40	Matthews, R.	33
Block, M.	2	McMillan, E.	5
Blunstone, F.	37	Mortimore, J.	33
Bonetti, P.	6	Nicholas, A.	7
Brabrook, P.	39	Robertson, W. G.	3
Bridges, B.	1	Scott, M.	9
Brooks, J.	20	Sillett, J.	21
Cliss, D.	4	Sillett, P.	41
Compton, J.	8	Shellito, K.	5
Corthine, P.	2	Tambling, R.	4
Crowther, S.	30	Tindall, R.	24
Gibbs, D.	4	Venables, T.	1
Greaves, J.	40	Whittaker, R.	8
Harrison, M.	5		

Goalscorers: Greaves 29, Livesey 9, Brabrook 7, Sillett, P. 6, Tindall 6, Blunstone 5, Brooks 5, Harrison 2, Allen 1, Anderton 1, Gibbs 1, Nicholas 1, Tambling 1, Opponents 2. **Total** 76.

Season 1960–61 (Div. I—12th)

P42, W15, D7, L20, Goals 98–100, Pts 37.

Appearances (22 Players)

Anderton, S.	22	Harris, A.	17
Block, M.	1	Harrison, M.	15
Blunstone, F.	24	Livesey, C.	14
Bonetti, P.	36	Matthews, R.	6
Brabrook, P.	36	Mortimore, J.	12
Bradbury, T.	15	Scott, M.	9
Bridges, B.	2	Sillett, J.	30
Brooks, J.	26	Sillett, P.	37
Evans, R.	32	Tambling, R.	24
Gibbs, D.	3	Tindall, R.	25
Greaves, J.	40	Venables, T.	36

Goalscorers: Greaves 41, Tindall 16, Tambling 9, Brabrook 8, Livesey 8, Blunstone 5, Sillett, P. 2, Anderton 1, Bradbury 1, Bridges 1, Brooks 1, Gibbs 1, Harrison 1, Mortimore 1, Opponents 2. **Total** 98.

Season 1961–62 (Div. I—22nd)

P42, W9, D10, L23, Goals 63–94, Pts 28.

Appearances (31 Players)

Anderton, S.	6	Moore, G.	17
Block, M.	1	Mortimore, J.	14
Blunstone, F.	26	Murray, A.	18
Bolland, G.	2	Pinner, M. J.	1
Bonetti, P.	33	Scott, M.	36
Brabrook, P.	37	Shaw, C.	1
Bradbury, T.	14	Shellito, K.	26
Bridges, B.	32	Sillett, J.	12
Butler, D.	16	Sillett, P.	3
Cliss, D.	8	Sorrell, D.	1
Docherty, T.	4	Tambling, R.	34
Harris, A.	27	Tindall, R.	5
Harris, R.	3	Upton, F.	10
Harrison, M.	22	Venables, T.	12
Malcolm, A.	27	Young, A.	6
McNally, E.	8		

Goalscorers: Tambling 20, Bridges 19, Brabrook 8, Murray 4, Harrison 3, Blunstone 2, Moore 2, Block 1, Malcolm 1, Venables 1, Opponents 2. **Total** 63.

Season 1962–63 (Div. II—2nd)

P42, W24, D4, L14, Goals 81–42, Pts 52.

Appearances (21 Players)

Blunstone, F.	34	McCreadie, E.	32
Bonetti, P.	39	Moore, G.	36
Bridges, B.	36	Mortimore, J.	42
Butler, D.	2	Mulholland, J.	4
Dunn, J.	3	Murray, A.	39
Harmer, T.	5	Shellito, K.	34
Harris, A.	15	Tambling, R.	40
Harris, R.	7	Upton, F.	37
Harrison, M.	1	Venables, T.	42
Kevan, D.	7	Watson, I.	1
Knox, T.	6		

Goalscorers: Tambling 35, Bridges 15, Blunstone 8, Moore 8, Murray 4, Upton 3, Venables 2, Harmer 1, Kevan 1, Mortimore 1, Mulholland 1, Opponents 2. **Total** 81.

Season 1963–64 (Div. I—5th)

P42, W20, D10, L12, Goals 72–56, Pts 50.

Appearances (24 Players)

Blunstone, F.	41	McCreadie, E.	35
Bonetti, P.	35	McNally, E.	1
Bridges, B.	33	Moore, G.	15
Brown, D.	10	Mortimore, J.	41
Dunn, J.	6	Mulholland, J.	7
Harmer, T.	3	Murray, A.	37
Harris, A.	10	Shellito, K.	18
Harris, R.	41	Sorrell, D.	2
Hinton, M.	21	Tambling, R.	35
Hollins, J.	2	Upton, F.	24
Houseman, P.	4	Venables, T.	38
Knox, T.	1	Watson, I.	2

Goalscorers: Tambling 17, Bridges 15, Murray 12, Venables 8, Blunstone 6, Moore 3, Harris, R. 2, Mortimore 2, Brown 1, Hinton 1, Houseman 1, McCreadie 1, Mulholland 1, Shellito 1, Watson 1. **Total** 72.

Season 1964–65 (Div. I—3rd)

P42, W24, D8, L10, Goals 89–54, Pts 56.

Appearances (22 Players)

Bonetti, P.	41	McCalliog, J.	3
Boyle, J.	6	McCreadie, E.	34
Bridges, B.	41	Murray, A.	40
Dunn, J.	1	Mortimore, J.	28
Graham, G.	30	Shellito, K.	13
Harris, A.	1	Sinclair, W.	1
Harris, R.	42	Smart, J.	1
Hinton, M.	40	Tambling, R.	33
Hollins, J.	41	Upton, F.	3
Houseman, P.	9	Venables, T.	39
Knox, T.	13	Watson, I.	2

Goalscorers: Bridges 20, Graham 17, Murray 17, Tambling 15, Venables 7, Harris, R. 2, Hollins 2, McCalliog 2, Mortimore 2, Hinton 1, Houseman 1, McCreadie 1, Shellito 1, Opponent 1. **Total** 89.

Season 1965–66 (Div. I—5th)

P42, W22, D7, L13, Goals 65–43, Pts 51.

Appearances (22 Players)

Barron, J.	1	Kirkup, J.	14
Bonetti, P.	38	McCalliog, J.	4
Boyle, J.	27 (3)	McCreadie, E.	30
Bridges, B.	27 (2)	Murray, A.	22 (4)
Dunn, J.	3	Osgood, P.	31 (1)
Fascione, J.	12 (3)	Robson, T.	6 (1)
Graham, G.	33	Shellito, K.	16
Harris, R.	36	Tambling, R.	26
Hinton, M.	38	Thomson, J.	2
Hollins, J.	39	Venables, T.	34
Houseman, P.	10	Young, A.	13

(Figures in brackets are appearances as substitute)

Goalscorers: Graham 17, Tambling 16, Bridges 9, Venables 8, Osgood 7, Harris 2, Hollins 2, Murray 2, Fascione 1, Kirkup 1. **Total** 65.

Season 1966–67 (Div. I—9th)

P42, W15, D14, L13, Goals 67–62, Pts 44.

Appearances (25 Players)

Baldwin, T.	30 (2)	Hughes, T.	2
Bonetti, P.	38	Kirkup, J.	24 (2)
Boyle, J.	36	Lloyd, B.	4
Cooke, C.	33	Luke, G.	1
Fascione, J.	4 (1)	McCreadie, E.	38
Graham, G.	9	Osgood, P.	10
Hamilton, I.	3 (2)	Stepney, A.	1
Harris, A.	12 (2)	Tambling, R.	36
Harris, R.	42	Thomson, J.	21 (4)
Hateley, A.	26 (1)	Whiffen, K.	1
Hinton, M.	38	Wosahlo, R.	– (1)
Hollins, J.	39	Young, A.	1
Houseman, P.	13 (5)		

(Figures in brackets are appearances as substitute)

Goalscorers: Tambling 21, Baldwin 16, Hateley 6, Osgood 6, Boyle 5, Cooke 3, Hamilton 2, Hollins 2, Graham 1, Houseman 1, Kirkup 1, McCreadie 1, Thomson 1, Opponent 1. **Total** 67.

Season 1967–68 (Div. I—6th)

P42, W18, D12, L12, Goals 62–68, Pts 48.

Appearances (22 Players)

Baldwin, T.	39	Houston, S.	1
Birchenall, A.	21	Hughes, T.	2
Bonetti, P.	40	Kirkup, J.	10 (3)
Boyle, J.	31 (1)	Lloyd, B.	1
Butler, G.	8 (1)	McCreadie, E.	36
Cooke, C.	41	McMillan, P.	1
Fascione, J.	6 (2)	Osgood, P.	42
Harris, R.	40	Tambling, R.	24
Hinton, M.	32 (1)	Thomson, J.	10 (2)
Hollins, J.	36	Waldron, C.	9
Houseman, P.	19 (1)	Webb, D.	13

(Figures in brackets are appearances as substitute)

Goalscorers: Osgood 16, Baldwin 15, Tambling 12, Birchenall 5, Boyle 4, Cooke 3, Houseman 3, Hollins 2, Opponents 2. **Total** 62.

Season 1968–69 (Div. I—5th)

P42, W20, D10, L12, Goals 73–53, Pts 50.

Appearances (20 Players)

Baldwin, T.	25	Houseman, P.	29 (3)
Birchenall, A.	39	Houston, S.	2
Bonetti, P.	41	Hudson, A.	1
Boyle, J.	33 (1)	Hughes, T.	1
Cooke, C.	25 (1)	Hutchinson, I.	14 (1)
Dempsey, J.	15	Lloyd, B.	3 (2)
Fascione, J.	– (1)	McCreadie, E.	38
Harris, R.	40	Osgood, P.	35
Hinton, M.	6 (3)	Tambling, R.	36 (2)
Hollins, J.	37	Webb, D.	42

(Figures in brackets are appearances as substitute)

Goalscorers: Tambling 17, Baldwin 16, Birchenall 12, Osgood 9, Hutchinson 6, Webb 6, Houseman 3, Hollins 2, Boyle 1, Opponent 1. **Total** 73.

Season 1969–70 (Div. I—3rd)

P42, W21, D13, L8, Goals 70–50, Pts 55.

Appearances (19 Players)

Baldwin, T.	17 (2)	Houston, S.	3 (3)
Birchenall, A.	14 (1)	Hudson, A.	29
Bonetti, P.	36	Hughes, T.	6
Boyle, J.	6 (1)	Hutchinson, I.	26 (1)
Cooke, C.	35	McCreadie, E.	29 (1)
Dempsey, J.	37	Mulligan, P.	6 (2)
Harris, R.	30	Osgood, P.	36 (2)
Hinton, M.	28	Tambling, R.	5 (2)
Hollins, J.	42	Webb, D.	35
Houseman, P.	42		

(Figures in brackets are appearances as substitute)

Goalscorers: Osgood 23, Hutchinson 16, Hollins 6, Baldwin 5, Cooke 4, Webb 4, Birchenall 3, Houseman 3, Hudson 3, Dempsey 2, Opponent 1. **Total** 70.

Season 1970–71 (Div. I—6th)

P42, W18, D15, L9, Goals 52–42, Pts 51.

Appearances (20 Players)

Baldwin, T.	18	Houseman, P.	36 (1)
Bonetti, P.	28	Hudson, A.	33 (1)
Boyle, J.	19 (1)	Hutchinson, I.	20
Cooke, C.	28 (3)	McCreadie, E.	13 (1)
Dempsey, J.	29 (2)	Mulligan, P.	16 (1)
Droy, M.	3 (1)	Osgood, P.	27
Feely, P.	2	Phillips, J.	14
Harris, R.	38	Smethurst, D.	12
Hinton, M.	20	Webb, D.	34
Hollins, J.	40	Weller, K.	32 (4)

(Figures in brackets are appearances as substitute)

Goalscorers: Weller 13, Hollins 6, Hutchinson 5, Osgood 5, Smethurst 4, Webb 4, Hudson 3, Baldwin 2, Houseman 2, Cooke 1, Dempsey 1, Feely 1, Harris 1, Mulligan 1, Opponents 3. **Total** 52.

Season 1971–72 (Div. 1—7th)

P42, W18, D12, L12, Goals 58–49, Pts 48.

Appearances (23 players)

Baldwin, T.	20	Hudson, A.	36
Bonetti, P.	33	Kember, S.	24 (3)
Boyle, J.	24	McCreadie, E.	7
Cooke, C.	35 (3)	Mulligan, P.	27
Dempsey, J.	35	Osgood, P.	36
Droy, M.	1	Phillips, J.	7
Feely, P.	– (1)	Potrac, A.	1
Garland, C.	16 (1)	Sherwood, S.	1
Harris, R.	41	Smethurst, D.	2
Hinton, M.	5 (1)	Webb, D.	41
Hollins, J.	42	Weller, K.	2
Houseman, P.	26 (1)		

(Figures in brackets are appearances as substitute).

Goalscorers: Osgood 18, Hollins 11, Baldwin 10, Garland 4, Webb 4, Kember 3, Cooke 2, Hudson 2, Dempsey 1, Houseman 1, Mulligan 1, Weller 1. **Total** 58.